The Best of
Holidays & Seasonal Celebrations
Arts & Crafts

A compilation of preK-3 issues 1-8,
preK-K issues 1-8, and grades 1-3 issues 13-21

Teaching & Learning Company

1204 Buchanan St., P.O. Box 10
Carthage, IL 62321-0010

D0910605

Edited and compiled by Donna Borst

Cover photo by Images and More Photography

Cover design by Jennifer Morgan

Illustrations by:

Elizabeth Adams	Shelly S. Rasche
Janet Armbrust	Mary Galan Rojas
Cara Bradshaw	Christina Schofield
Gary Hoover	Veronica Terrill
Becky Radtke	Gayle Vella

Copyright © 2001, Teaching & Learning Company

ISBN No. 1-57310-280-6

Printing No. 987654321

Teaching & Learning Company
1204 Buchanan St., P.O. Box 10
Carthage, IL 62321-0010

At the time of publication every effort was made to insure the accuracy of the information included in this book. However, we cannot guarantee that agencies and organizations mentioned will continue to operate or to maintain these current locations.

This book belongs to

_____

Contributors:

Cindy Barden
Carol Ann Bloom
Amanda Boor
Jo Jo Cavalline
Marie E. Cecchini
Elaine Hansen Cleary
Tania Kourempis-Cowling
Ann Curtis
Robynne Eagan
Susan Jordan
Mary Maurer

Sister M. Yvonne Moran
Jo Anne O'Donnell
Diana M. Schmitt
Carol Smallwood
Maria B. Smith
E.E. Stewart
Donna Stringfellow
Carolyn Ross Tomlin
Mary Tucker
Judy Wolfman
D.A. Woodliff
Rose Ross Zediker

Table of Contents

TLC10280 Copyright © Teaching & Learning Company, Carthage, IL 62321-0010

Spring 85

Summer 107

Dear Teacher or Parent,

Welcome to a new kind of compilation of the best of the the best of *Holidays & Seasonal Celebrations* magazines. This time we have gathered the very best arts and crafts activities that we have to offer and compiled them into one big, easy-to-use resource for your convenience. We think you'll be pleased with what we've chosen. We want to thank every author, illustrator, and teacher who contributed to this book. Without them none of this would be possible.

We've divided these activities by season, and you'll be amazed, and happy, to discover the variety of crafts available for many holidays and all seasons of the year.

For fall, you'll find back-to-school ideas such as personalized pencil cases and school folders to help students start the year in an organized way. We've also provided art activities and crafts to celebrate Grandparents' Day, Columbus Day, and Halloween. Your students will also enjoy the crafts that make use of nature's autumn products such as leaves, seeds, and nuts.

To add interest to your winter classroom, try some of the snowmen crafts included as well as ideas for Book Week, Thanksgiving (using gourds, pinecones, weeds, and corn), Hanukkah, Christmas, Kwanzaa, New Year's, and, of course, Valentine's Day. We've also included some creative ideas for reusing Christmas cards.

Spring into spring with the crafts we've provided for St. Patrick's Day and Earth Day as well as April Fools' hats, Easter bunnies, baskets and bonnets, and fun egg projects.

For summer, your students will enjoy crafts for May Day and Cinco de Mayo, gifts for Mother's Day and Father's Day, and patriotic crafts for Flag Day and July 4th. You'll also find fun crafts to celebrate summer with butterflies and watermelon.

These arts and crafts are not only fun; they're educational! Your students will learn about famous people and events, the natural world, and much more as they work on these projects individually and in groups. And most of the activities in this book require only basic arts and crafts materials such as paper; scissors; glue; paints; crayons; containers, such as jars and boxes; and natural items that can be gathered from most yards or parks.

We hope you enjoy all the activities we've gathered for you; we know your students will!

Sincerely,

Donna Borst

Donna Borst

If you would like to contribute to future issues of *Holidays & Seasonal Celebrations*, please direct your submissions to:

Teaching & Learning Company
Holidays & Seasonal Celebrations
1204 Buchanan St., P.O. Box 10
Carthage, IL 62321-0010

Back-to-School

Personalized Pencil Case

Here is a project to help cure the lost pencil syndrome. Personal pencil cases are handy to use, cannot be confused with another classmate's, and are colorful enough to find in any desk.

Supplies

felt, ruler, chalk, glitter, Velcro™, scissors, glue

Instructions

1. Have each child measure and cut two rectangles, one 3" x 7" and one 3" x 9", from felt. Use chalk to draw the cutting lines.

2. Let them write their names on the smaller rectangle with glue, then sprinkle glitter over the glue. Allow glue to dry.

3. Have children place glue around three edges (two long, one short) on the back of the smaller rectangle. Top with the second rectangle, matching bottom corners. Press the glued edges together.

4. Finally, turn the pencil case back over to the front side and glue Velcro™ pieces to the top centers of both rectangles. Allow the glue to dry before closing.

Use: Children can slide their pencils into the long pocket, fold over the top flap, and press the Velcro™ pieces together to "lock" the case. Individual pencil cases help children keep track of their writing materials and keep pencils from rolling out of desks.

by Marie E. Cecchini

Dog Week Dalmatians

Creative crafting encourages children to view ordinary things from a different perspective. Showing them how to reuse cardboard tubes with this Dalmatian project will start their creative juices flowing. What other projects can they envision making with cardboard tubes?

Supplies

bath tissue tubes, white tempera paint, felt scraps in white and black, large black pom-poms, black tissue paper, paintbrushes, markers, scissors, glue

Instructions

1. Each child will need one and a half bath tissue tubes. Let children paint their tubes white.

2. Have children cut and glue black felt "spots" to the large tube; then glue four black pom-pom legs/feet to one side to make a Dalmatian body. Set the body on its legs, then glue the half tube to the top to create a head. If necessary, use a clothespin to hold the head in place until the glue dries.

3. To complete the head, have children draw, cut, and glue on white felt ears, crumpled tissue paper eyes and nose, and black felt spots. Use a marker to add spots to the ears.

4. Cut and glue a white felt tail to the opposite end of the tube.

Use: Have children name their dogs; then write a story about their pets. You may want to discuss pet owner responsibilities and ways in which dogs help us.

Apple Beanbags

Sing "Happy Birthday" to Johnny Appleseed; then invite your students to create apples of their own for developing motor coordination and skills.

Supplies

red, brown and green felt scraps, rice or beans, glue, scissors, chalk

Instructions

1. Have children use chalk to draw two circles on red felt. You may want to prepare cardboard patterns so the circles will be large enough and of uniform shape. Have children cut these circles out.

2. Have children draw and cut out brown stems to glue at the top of one red circle. Have children draw a line of glue around the edge of this circle, leaving a 1" space unglued. Top with the second red circle and press the glued edges together.

3. Let children draw and cut out one or two green felt leaves to place on the front of the apple near the stem. Glue these in place and allow the glue to dry.

4. Help children partially fill their apples with rice or dried beans. You may want to roll a piece of paper into a funnel shape to make the job easier. Afterward, glue the open section closed and allow glue to dry.

Use: Johnny Appleseed is usually portrayed using a pot for a hat. Let younger children take turns tossing their beanbags into a large pot. With older children, use several numbered pots. Have children throw three or four beanbags; then add up their total number of points.

Back-to-School Name Bracelets

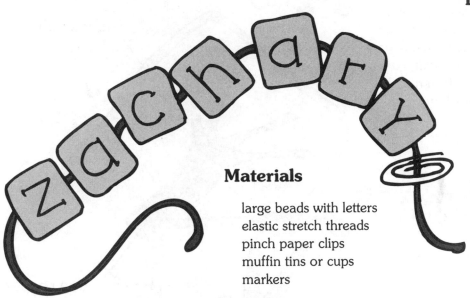

Materials

large beads with letters
elastic stretch threads
pinch paper clips
muffin tins or cups
markers

Let's Make It

1. Label the letter name on the outside of the cups.

2. Have children help put the letter beads in the appropriate cups.

3. Have children take an empty cup and fill it with the letters of their name.

4. Help children attach a pinch clip to one end of their bracelet string as a holder.

5. Children may need assistance to thread the letter beads on the string in the correct order, holding the free end up so the beads do not fall from it.

6. Once all the letters have been threaded, the paper clip can be removed and the ends tied together to form a bracelet. Children may need assistance.

Harvest Moon

This is a glow-in-the-dark harvest delight. In Chinese tradition the moon is thought to symbolize perfect joy and the cycle of life.

Materials

white construction paper
gray paint
small sponges and paint bowls
glow-in-the-dark paint
tagboard circle or wooden moon shape to trace
pencils
scissors

Let's Make It

1. Have children trace the moon shape onto the construction paper, and then cut out the shape.

2. Instruct children to dip the sponge into a bowl, and then dab it onto their moon shape.

3. When the gray paint dries, children can sponge phosphorescent paint over their moon.

Try This

Pull the blinds to darken your classroom. Have children hold their moon shapes up to the lights for 30 to 60 seconds. Turn off the lights and have children wave their harvest moons in the air.

by Robynne Eagan

Dot Trees

Colorful leaves are a natural part of the fall experience in many areas. Help your children explore this event by making colorful wall hangings.

Supplies

cardboard boxes, brown construction paper, colorful construction paper scraps, yarn, paper punch, glue

Instructions

1. Tear cardboard boxes apart, creating various sizes and shapes.

2. Have children rip brown construction paper pieces to create a simple tree shape. Instruct them to glue these trees to a cardboard piece.

3. Have children use a paper punch to make dots in various colors, spread glue over their trees, then sprinkle the colors over the glue.

4. Punch two holes at the top of each picture. Thread yarn through the holes and knot to create a hanger.

Activities

Name the colors and parts of a tree. Discuss why some trees lose their leaves in the fall. Repeat this tree project for each season. Have children imagine they are trees in autumn. How would they feel and what would they think about this seasonal change? Write a class story from the viewpoint of the tree.

cardboard

tree shapes

glue

paper punch dots

Jose's Tree

by Marie Cecchini

10

School Folders

Individual school folders can help children become better organized. Less time spent searching for misplaced items leaves more time for learning.

Supplies

manila folders   markers
stickers   stamps and stamp pads
glue

Instructions

1. Each child will need one manila folder and a 5" strip cut lengthwise from a second folder.

2. Have children write their names on the folder tabs, then open their folders flat. Demonstrate how to lay the manila strip across the bottom of the folder, then glue around the edges to secure. This creates a pocket on each side of the folder.

3. Let children use markers, stickers, stamps and stamp pads to decorate the outside of their folders.

Activity

Encourage children to learn about responsibility by having them use these folders on a daily basis for transporting homework and important messages between school and home.

Family Garland

Get to know your students, and help them get to know each other with a different kind of family portrait.

Supplies

construction paper in various colors, gingerbread person cookie cutter, crayons or markers, scissors, glue

Instructions

1. Have each child trace and cut a construction paper person for each family member, including themselves. You can use paper in multicultural shades or simply use a variety of colors.

2. Instruct children to add facial features and clothing to each family member; then glue the people together as if they were holding hands.

Activities

Encourage children to share the garlands with the class and invite them to tell something about each family member. Prompt them with questions as necessary, and encourage the class to ask questions. Display these families on a bulletin board for parent night or open house.

by Marie Cecchini

11

Color Mobile

This simple mobile project invites children to learn color names, read color name words and practice alphabetical order.

Supplies

one box of eight crayons per child, 8" cardboard tubes, construction paper in the same eight colors, yarn in eight colors, glue, scissors

Instructions

1. Prepare 1" paper strips in each of the eight colors.

2. Have children choose one paper strip in each color; then glue the strips side by side around their cardboard tubes. Challenge older children to alphabetize the color names before they glue on their strips.

3. Instruct children to cut a length of yarn for each crayon. Have them find and read the color word on each crayon as they match colors; then help them tie one end of each yarn length to the appropriate crayon. Secure each knot with a dot of glue. Tie the opposite ends of each yarn length to the cardboard tube, matching colors. Again, secure the knots with glue.

4. To make a hanger, cut a longer length of yarn, thread it through the entire length of the tube and knot the ends together.

Activities

Have the children use their mobiles to answer questions such as, "Which color name begins with *y* (r, b, p and so on)?" "Who can name the letters that spell *green* (red, orange and so on)?," and "Show me which two colors we would mix together to make purple?" Encourage children to share their color knowledge with their families when they bring their mobiles home.

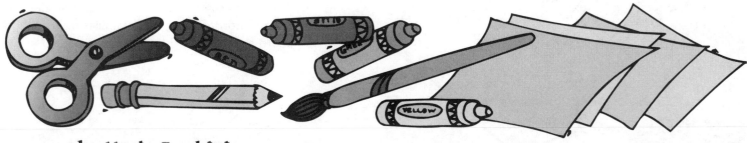

by Marie Cecchini

Good Citizen Award

Citizenship Day, September 17

Advance Preparation: Cut a 3" circle for each child (any color). Punch two holes in the top of each circle. Make a star pattern that fits inside the circle. Cut a 4" yellow square for each child. Cut a 30" piece of yarn for each child. Put glitter in saltshakers so that it is easier for children to use.

Get

any color circle

star pattern

yellow paper

scissors

glue

yarn

marker

glitter

Do

1. Trace.

2. Cut.

3. Lace yarn.

4. Glue.

5. Glue and glitter.

6. Good Citizen Award

by Carol Ann Bloom

Grandparent Spooners

Create special gifts for Grandparents' Day using small wooden craft or ice cream spoons. Making gifts for family members and friends encourages children to think of others.

Supplies

wooden craft or ice cream spoons, pipe cleaners, yarn, fabric and felt scraps, fine line markers, pin backs and/or magnetic strips, scissors, glue

Instructions

1. Let children count and choose spoons to match the number of grandparents they have; then use fine line markers to add facial features.

2. Prepare pipe cleaners in both 2" and 4" lengths. Have children wrap a 4" pipe cleaner around their spoons, just below the head, for arms and secure with glue. Let them glue two 2" pipe cleaners at the bottom for legs. When the glue dries, they can bend the pipe cleaner ends to make hands and feet.

3. Instruct children to create clothing using felt and fabric scraps, and yarn hair. Help children glue these to the spoon in appropriate places. Then glue a pin back or magnetic strip to the back of each spoon.

Use: As children complete their projects, have them each contribute a statement for you to write on a large chart titled *What I Like About My Grandparents.* Older students may write their own. Wrap the pin/magnet gifts to take home for Grandparents' Day.

Ruler Bookmarks

September is the month for Literacy Day and Library Card Sign Up. Stimulate interest in reading and books in general by crafting special bookmarks and highlighting the importance of learning to read.

Supplies

teacher-prepared paper rulers, cardboard, markers, glue

Instructions

1. Make use of a 12" ruler and copy machine to photocopy a paper ruler for each child. Cut cardboard strips.

2. Have each child glue a paper ruler to a cardboard strip, trimming the cardboard as necessary.

3. Have younger children mark off each inch with a red marker. Let each older child mark off inches in red, half inches in blue. Have both groups write *Reading Rules* across their bookmarks.

Use: Have children choose books from either the school or classroom library to use with their bookmarks. Send a short note home to parents encouraging them to help their children obtain and use library cards. Invite children to brainstorm 12 ideas (for 12 inches) about how reading helps us. Challenge them to become aware of reading opportunities and the necessity of reading in daily experiences such as reading signs, recipes, game directions, and so on. Have children share their observations with the class.

by Marie Cecchini

"Write" on, Grandparents

Grandparents' Day Cards

Set aside some time early in the week for students to make special cards for grandparents. Using markers, colored pencils, or paints, instruct students to fold and then illustrate these special cards. Ask students to copy one of the following verses on the cards or write one of their own.

North, South, East, or West,
Grandpa (Grandma), you're just the best!

Roses are red; violets are blue!
Grandma (Grandpa), I love you!

After the cards are completed, have students copy their grandparents' address to complete the envelope. Mail the cards to each grandparent. Parents might donate envelopes or stamps to help defray mailing costs.

Grandparent Quilt

Stitch together students' best memories of grandparents by creating a paper quilt. Give each student a 6" square of white paper. Instruct them to draw a favorite memory or occasion they experienced with their grandparents. Ask older students to write about the memory when the square is done. To make the classroom quilt, mount each white square in the middle of a 7" x 7" square of colored construction paper. Punch a hole about every inch along each side of the square. Next, lay out the squares on the floor and arrange them in rows until the pictures, colors, and patterns are pleasing. If there is an uneven row, fill it in with one to three squares giving the title of the quilt, class name, and year. Take a length of yarn and lace the squares together. Display your quilt on a wall of the school.

by Terry Healy

TLC10280 Copyright © Teaching & Learning Company, Carthage, IL 62321-0010

Grandparents Are Great!

Remember grandparents on their special day with
this heartfelt message.

Materials

red construction paper
(large heart drawn or copied on it)
photocopied or printed tag reading
Grandparents Are Great!
glue or glue sticks
scissors
markers, pencils, or crayons

Setup

Provide materials at center. Ask the questions, "What makes your
grandparents special? What do you like to do with your grandparents?"

Let's Make It

1. Instruct children to cut out the heart and draw a picture of themselves doing a favorite activity with their grandparents.

2. Have children paste the printed tag somewhere on the heart.

Try This

More than one visit to the center
may be needed to recognize
all grandparents.

by Robynne Eagan

Leaf Prints

Materials

leaf, fern, or flower
two panes of Plexiglas™
thick pad of newspaper
white printing paper
oil-based ink
thin foam paint roller to spread the ink
firm paint roller to apply pressure
clean-up rags and turpentine

Let's Make It

1. Take a nature hike to collect some interesting leaves. The leaves should be flat and not too dry or delicate.

2. Cover a work area with newspaper or vinyl. Have participants cover their clothing with aprons or shirts.

3. Apply a small amount of ink to the plastic pane, and have the child roll the roller over the ink until the pane is evenly coated with ink.

4. Have children place their leaves on a flat, newspaper-coated surface. Roll the inked roller over the leaf until the leaf is coated with ink.

5. Carefully lift the leaf and place it ink-side up on the clean pane.

6. Place the white paper on top of the leaf with a steady hand. The paper and the leaf must remain perfectly still once they touch.

7. Have the child place a thin pad of newspaper over the printing paper, and tape the newspaper to the corners of the pane.

8. Roll a clean roller back and forth over the paper with firm pressure.

9. Carefully remove the newspaper, and then lift the printing paper from the leaf. Place the paper on a flat surface or hang to dry.

10. Clean the roller, hands, and plastic pane before the ink dries. Turpentine will remove the ink but can be dangerous. Use as little as needed in a supervised setting. Ensure that children wash their hands thoroughly with soap and water.

Discuss the leaves and the prints. What makes each leaf unique? Which leaves are from trees? Which are from plants? Can students identify the plants or the trees? Take a look at the veins. What do the veins do?

by Robynne Eagan

17

Scarecrow Steve

Autumn wouldn't be complete without a raggy, baggy scarecrow. Use the patterns on page 19 with your children and have them make their own whirly, twirly scarecrows to hang. After children color and cut out the pieces, help them tape each piece separately to a long piece of string or yarn. Begin near the top of the string and tape the hat on first. Leave a space, then tape the head on. Proceed in the same manner with the shirt and the pants. Make a loop at the top for hanging, and watch the scarecrow dance.

by Marie Cecchini

Fun with Fall

Fall Tree

Draw a tree trunk on white construction paper. Color the trunk brown with crayons. With a hole punch, make dots of red, orange, yellow and brown paper. Glue these on the tree limbs and all around the base of the tree. There are several variations you can use on this tree:

- Sponge-paint leaves.
- Glue on small squares in fall colors.
- Glue on crumpled wads of colored tissue paper.

Leaf Prints Using Paint

With a brush, paint red, orange and yellow tempera paint onto the front sides of leaves. Press the painted side onto paper. For a variation, place the paint on the back side of the leaf and press down—you might see more distinct markings on this print.

Leaves in Plastic

Place your leaves on the sticky side of clear self-adhesive plastic. Cover with another sheet of plastic and press. Cut around the leaves, punch holes in them and thread yarn or ribbon for a leaf hanging. Or cut a single leaf and use it as a bookmark.

by Tania Kourempis-Cowling

Nutty Wind Chime

Tree seeds, or nuts, are plentiful in the fall. Help your child use some nuts to make a wind chime; then listen for the special sound it makes. First, have your youngster color a design on a bathroom tissue tube. Thread a length of yarn or string through the tube and knot the ends together to create a hanger. Next, help your child wrap and glue one end of a length of ribbon around each nut you choose to use. Wrap and glue the opposite end of each ribbon around the cardboard tube. Allow the glue to dry; then hang it where it will catch the breeze but not the raindrops.

by Marie Cecchini

Leaf People

Place leaves under sheets of white paper. Rub the sides of red, orange, and yellow crayons on paper over leaves until leaf shapes appear. Cut out leaf shapes and paste them to background paper. Add heads, arms, and legs. Encourage students to have the leaf people engaged in some activity. Display some of the leaf shapes with the names of their trees.

by Mabel Duch

Columbus Day Craft

Here's a quick and easy craft your students can make during the month of October to help celebrate Columbus Day. Each child will need a large, white sheet of construction paper; one half of a paper plate; a sheet of white paper; three craft sticks; one paper fastener; a reproducible Columbus pattern (provided); tape; glue; crayons and scissors. Now just follow the steps below to create a ship that really rocks back and forth!

1. Cut paper plates in half so that each child has one half.
2. To make the ship, color the back side brown. Write *Columbus Day and the year* on it.
3. Cut two squares and a triangle from the sheet of white photocopy paper. Glue each onto a craft stick to make sails.
4. Color and cut out the Columbus pattern.
5. Tape the sails and Columbus onto the back of the ship.
6. Lay the sheet of white construction paper horizontally and color the bottom third to look like the sea. Draw some clouds in the sky.
7. Position the ship onto the sea. Push a paper fastener through the bottom of the ship and the construction paper.
8. Pretend Columbus is sailing on his voyage to America. For added fun, hold the edge of the ship and gently move it up and down.

COLUMBUS PUPPET

Color and cut out. Match the dots. Attach arms and legs with brads.

by Carolyn Tomlin

Celebrating Columbus Day

Walnut Ship

Use half of a walnut shell for the ship. Place playdough in the bottom of the ship. Glue a triangular-shaped sail made of construction paper or fabric to a toothpick. Stick the toothpick into the playdough. Sail the ship in a pan of water, navigating it by blowing on the sail. What happens if there is no wind? Too much wind?

Three Ships Mural

Draw three large ships on a sheet of mural paper. Let the children cooperatively color the ships brown. Have each child draw their own mast on one of the ships—a unique drawing of their own. At circle time, have each student show their individual mast and discuss their drawing and its meaning.

This is also a good time to sing songs such as "Row, Row, Row Your Boat"; "Merrily We Roll Along" and "Blow the Man Down," just to name a few.

by Tania Kourempis-Cowling

The Ocean Blue

Have the children feel the rhythm of the ocean as they make a finger painting of the sea that Christopher Columbus sailed. Provide blue finger paint and paper; then encourage the kids to make lots of wavy lines.

Ship in a Bottle Art

Cut a sheet of white construction paper into a bottle shape. Have the children draw Columbus' ships sailing the ocean blue. Draw some sea life in the water and a view of land in the distance. Make the drawings colorful with bright crayons or markers. When finished, cover the entire drawing with clear cellophane wrap. Use tape to secure the plastic. This gives the illusion of the boats in a bottle.

Columbus Day Garland

Children can use construction paper to draw and cut out pictures of boats, flags, telescopes and maps. Attach these to crepe paper streamers and use as garlands to decorate doors, windows and to drape along the ceiling.

United Nations Day Flag

October 24 is a day to celebrate peace and reflect on the diversity of the many people of the world.

Materials

straws
11" x 17" white paper
writing and/or painting instruments
stapler and staples

Setup

Prepare a blank sample flag to illustrate how the flag is made. Prepare a center providing the materials listed above.

Discussion

The United Nations organization was founded on October 24, 1945. This group of nations works together to promote peace around the world. Today over 150 nations are members of this organization. Is your country a member? What harm is caused by violent conflicts between nations? How might nations resolve conflicts? How does it make you feel to know that many nations have united together to try to achieve worldwide peace?

Let's Make It

1. Use the sample to help you explain how the paper is wrapped around the straw and folded in half.

2. Staple the folded side of the paper, anchoring the paper to the straw.

3. Run cellophane tape around the edges of the flag to secure the two sides together.

4. Decorate both sides of the flag to represent world peace.

Try This

Display the flags on a bulletin board or along a border with a background of blue skies and white clouds. Center your display around the words *United Nations for Worldwide Peace.*

by Robynne Eagan

Halloween Mask on a Stick

Materials

- scissors
- white glue and glue sticks
- small paper plates
- masking tape
- wide craft sticks
- construction paper
- wool
- markers, crayons and pencils
- stickers
- pasta shapes

Let's Make It

1. Make a sample mask on a stick and display it for students.

2. Have children glue a small paper plate onto a wide craft stick.

3. Instruct them to decorate their masks using markers, crayons or pencils; stickers; pasta shapes and so on.

by Robynne Eagan

Ghostly Pencil Toppers

Materials

- pencils (orange, black, white or Halloween themed)
- white tissues
- fine tip black marker
- rubber bands

Let's Make It

1. Prepare a sample model to display.

2. Have students layer two tissues flat on their desktops.

3. Next, crumple two or more tissues to form a ball.

4. Have children place the ball on top of their pencil, and then use the double layer of flat tissue to wrap around the ball and over the pencil.

5. Wrap a rubber band around the base of the ball and the flat tissues.

6. Have students draw a ghostly face on the tissue with black marker.

by Robynne Eagan

Ghostly Creations

Fill your classroom with ghostly puff creations made with popped corn. First, have the children cut ghostly shapes from cereal box cardboard. Make a hole at the top of each and thread with string for hanging. Next, provide the children with plastic lids to hold glue and popped corn. Have them dip each piece of popped corn into the glue; then stick the popcorn onto one side of their shapes, covering the cardboard. Allow the glue to dry, then proceed in the same manner to cover the back side of the shapes. Have children cut black eye and mouth shapes and glue them on one side. When dry, suspend the ghostly creations from the ceiling, or bring in a small branch from the playground and create a Halloween tree.

by Marie Cecchini

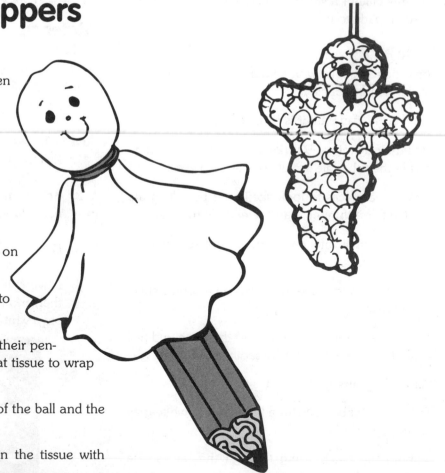

Boney Knockers

Materials
play clay
drinking straws
pencils
paintbrushes
black and white acrylic paint
black shoelaces, wool, or elasticized thread

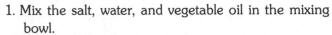

Setup
Make Play Clay
$3/4$ cup salt (175 ml)
$3/4$ cup water (175 ml)
1 tsp. (ml) vegetable oil
2 cups (500 ml) flour
large mixing bowl

1. Mix the salt, water, and vegetable oil in the mixing bowl.
2. Add the flour, a little at a time, and mix until the mixture forms a ball.
3. Knead the ball of dough for about 10 minutes.
4. Store the clay in a sealed container in the refrigerator until ready to use.

Let's Make It

1. Provide each child with a flour-dusted work surface and a handful of clay.

2. Knead the clay until it is soft, warm, and pliable.

3. Roll the clay into a $3/4$" (2 cm) thick tube, and then divide the tube into small bone-sized pieces.

4. Shape the pieces to look like bones by rolling the middle to be thinner than the ends of the piece.

5. Press a pencil into each end of the roll to form indentations.

6. Use a spatula to place the bones on a cookie sheet for drying.

7. Push a straw top into one end of the bone and pull it out to make a hole for threading string through.

8. Allow 48 hours for the bones to dry.

9. Paint the dry bones with a light coat of white-gray acrylic paint.

10. Thread the black string through the bones. Tie each bone in place to form a string of bones to hang from a door or ceiling.

Swinging Spiders

Materials
black pipe cleaners
thread or string

Let's Make It
1. Have children bend black pipe cleaners into spider shapes. How many legs should each have?

2. Children can tie or wrap the string around the spider, leaving a long end of string coming from the center of the spider. Hang the spiders from the ceiling, door frame, or door knocker or add to a Spooky Spiderweb.

Spooky Spiderwebs

Materials
box or tray with sides at least 2" (5 cm) high
black construction paper cut to fit in the box
white paint in a squirt bottle
marbles

Let's Make It
1. Place a piece of black construction paper inside the tray.

2. Add a small puddle of white paint in the center or corners of the paper.

3. Drop a marble (or two) in the box.

4. Have children tip the tray gently, raising one side and then another to roll the marbles through the paint to create a white spiderweb.

by Robynne Eagan

26

Haunted Houses

Here is a Halloween art project that students love to make! Use the "haunted houses" for a seasonal display in the hallway or your classroom.

Using chalk, draw an outline of a haunted house or mansion on black construction paper. A pattern is provided on page 29. The bigger the house, the better! Next create windows with shutters by drawing a capital *I* in every spot a window is desired. A capital *T* can be drawn for a double door entry at ground level, or an upside down *L* for a single door. After doors and windows are placed, have children cut on the chalk lines to make the windows and doors open. It is important to "open" all windows and doors before continuing. Have children cut out the entire house. Instruct them to carefully apply glue to the house, avoiding the openings. Glue the house onto a contrasting piece of uncut construction paper of the same or larger size.

Next instruct children to draw and cut out seasonal things to place behind the doors and windows. When the shutters are opened, the spooky surprises are revealed. Some suggestions for surprises to place behind the shutters are jack-o'-lanterns, bats, skeletons, witches, owls, monsters, ghosts, and black cats. Clip art is provided on the following page.

Finally create an outdoor scene around the house. Children could draw graveyards, a moon, dead trees, and so on.

Simplify this project for younger children by making only the shutters. Use a contrasting background paper and black or brown paper for the shutters to make a spooky window. Cut one piece of 9" x 12" paper in half for the shutters. Glue to the right and left edges of contrasting background paper. Instruct children to make a jack-o'-lantern or other spooky item to place inside the shutters.

Display the following poem with the completed project and encourage interaction.

> *If you're afraid of monsters*
> *That growl and grin,*
> *Don't open our shutters!*
> *Don't look in!*

by Karen K. Bjork

Pumpkin Projects

Quick and Easy Jack-O'-lantern Projects Everyone Can Make

Pencil Topper or Finger Puppet

Provide children with orange paper rectangles measuring 2" x 4", scissors, markers, glue, and pipe cleaners. Demonstrate how to fold the rectangle in half, forming a 2" square.

Next show how to draw a pumpkin on the square with one side of the pumpkin at the fold. Instruct children to draw and cut out these pumpkin shapes. Remind them not to cut on the fold. The pumpkins should open and close like a book.

With the pumpkins folded, have children design different faces on the front and back. Instruct children to open their pumpkins and place a dab of glue in the center of one. Have them lay one end of a pipe cleaner into the glue; then fold the pumpkin closed over the pipe cleaner. Instruct children to gently press the sides together; then allow the glue to dry. When dry, wrap the pipe cleaner stem around a pencil for a topper, or around a finger for a puppet.
Note: If the tip of any pipe cleaner is sharp, cover with tape.

Doorknob Hanger/Noisemaker

For this project, each child will need two small paper plates, orange paint, paper scraps, markers, scissors, and glue.

First, have children paint the back of each plate orange. Allow the paint to dry, then instruct children to create facial features out of paper scraps to glue on one plate.

Staple each pair of plates together, leaving a small opening at the top. Let each child drop a few beans, one by one, into the opening, counting as they drop. Insert a green rectangle stem into each opening, and staple closed.

Use a hole punch to pierce a hole on each side of the stem. Thread and tie a length of yarn through the holes for hanging. Use the yarn to suspend the jack-o'-lanterns from a doorknob or to shake them as musical instruments.

by Marie Cecchini

Coffee Can Banks

Cut orange paper rectangles (about 5" x 14") to cover 10-13 oz. coffee cans. Have children remove the plastic lids from the cans, then help them wrap the cans with the paper, securing the paper with tape.

Instruct children to design and cut out facial features and stems from scrap paper. Provide glue and have children add the facial features to the front of their cans, with the stem at the top. Use a knife or scissors to cut a coin slot in the lid of each child's bank.

Variation: Not enough coffee cans? Try the same procedure using icing containers.

Tissue Paper Jack-O'-Lanterns

For each child, bend a wire coat hanger into a circular shape. Or have them bring in the circle-shaped hangers from home. Have children lay their hangers on a large sheet of orange tissue paper. Show them how to "trace" the hanger with glue, so the glue runs onto the tissue paper.

Top each hanger with a second sheet of tissue paper. Allow the glue to dry, then use scissors to remove the excess tissue paper, creating an orange circle. Let children use paper scraps, markers, scissors, and glue to add facial features to their jack-o'-lanterns.

Instruct children to wrap the hooks with green crepe paper streamers, securing the paper with tape to create a stem.

Variation: For smaller jack-o'-lanterns, simply shape a smaller circle with a hook out of sturdy wire.

Wind Sock

Let children use paper scraps, glue, markers, and scissors to create a jack-o'-lantern face on 9" x 12" sheets of orange paper. Roll each paper into a cylinder and fasten with staples or tape. Use a hole punch to pierce a hole in each side of the top of the cylinder. Thread yarn through the holes and tie to make a hanger. Help children tape three crepe paper streamers to the inside bottom of their cylinders.

Happy/Scary Stick Puppet

Have each child draw (or trace), color, and cut out a medium-sized pumpkin shape from orange paper. One one side, ask them to design a happy jack-o'-lantern, on the reverse side, a scary one. Tape these pumpkins to craft sticks and invite children to tell why their jack-o'-lanterns are happy. Discuss what makes the other faces scary. Prompt them to conclude that masks are only pretend.

Wrist Decor

Slice cardboard tubes into 2" pieces, one for each child. Slit each piece to open like a bracelet. Provide children with strips of orange paper to glue around their cardboard pieces. Have them draw, color, and cut small jack-o'-lanterns from orange scrap paper; then glue their designs to the fronts of their bracelets. Older children may enjoy creating the same project using orange felt instead of paper.

Spooky Spiders

Create some spooky eight-legged creepy crawlies for Halloween.

Jane

Materials

black plasticine or modeling clay
eight black pipe cleaner segments for
    each child
flat work surface
name tags or labeled work surface

Setup

Separate the plasticine or clay into walnut-sized pieces, one for each child. Cut pipe cleaners into 1" pieces for spider legs.

by Robynne Eagan

Write each child's name on a name tag or piece of paper for identification. Ask "How many legs does a spider have? Let's count to eight together."

Let's Make It

1. Instruct children to make a spider body out of the plasticine and then attach the legs by poking them into the body.
2. Display the finished products on a name tag or paper with the child's name.

Frosty & Friends

Heat up the long, cold days of winter with some exciting snowpeople activities and projects.

Designer Snowpeople

Prepare several pairs of poster board white snowpeople. To each pair, add identical hat and scarf designs made of wall-paper or wrapping paper, matching sequin buttons, and marker facial features. To use with the group, have each child pull one snowperson from the bag, then have the children pair themselves to match. To use independently, place all of the snowpeople into a shoe box or basket for children to match at free time.

Jumbo Snowpeople

Help children draw and cut out three large white circles and a giant-sized black hat. Have them glue their shapes together to make life-size snowpeople. Let them add a fabric scrap scarf, real button eyes, and square felt "coal" buttons. Make use of one snowperson to dramatize the story of "Frosty the Snowman" then display them around the room.

Bookmark

Reading is a wonderful winter pastime. Create an interest in reading with snowpeople bookmarks. Have children paint tongue depressors or craft sticks white, then use fine-point markers to add facial features. Help them cut felt hats and scarves to glue above and below the face. Check out snowy day books at the library. The bookmark can also double as a puppet.

Frosty Crayon Cup

Have children use tape and white paper to cover a recycled icing container. Provide them with scrap paper, markers, glue, and scissors for transforming this plain white cup into a snowperson head by adding a face. Use the finished cups for holding crayons, scissors, markers, and pencils.

by Marie E. Cecchini

Window Square

Provide each child with a 9" square of blue paper. Demonstrate how to fold the paper in half, matching corners. Then show how to draw half of a snowperson against the folded side. Have children cut out the shapes, holding their papers folded, then open the papers to reveal a complete snowperson shape. On the back of the original paper, tape or glue a piece of waxed paper over the snowperson shape. On the front, add glitter facial features and buttons. Then cut out and glue a paper hat above the head. Tape the ends of a length of yarn to each top corner, then hang in a window.

Lid Plaque

Collect jar lids of various sizes and prepare a rectangle of corrugated cardboard for each child. To make snowperson plaques, have children choose three lids in graduated sizes and glue them to the cardboard. Have them cover each lid with glue, then place popped corn into the glue, filling each lid. Provide markers, scissors, and scrap paper for them to add facial features and a hat to the top lid, and a scarf and buttons to the second lid. Frame each plaque with popped corn and add a yarn loop on the back for hanging.

Three-Ring Mobile

Provide children with black and white scrap paper, white paper strips, markers, scissors, glue or tape, and yarn. Have them draw and cut out a black hat, then tape a loop of yarn to the top for hanging. For the head, let them shape a paper strip into a ring. Attach this with yarn below the hat. Next, cut a circle of white, add marker facial features, then hang inside of head ring with yarn. Shape two additional white strip rings and attach them below the head with yarn to create a snowperson.

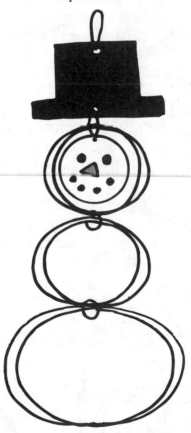

Mittens for

Left and Right

Enhance your students' knowledge of left and right with a pretty mitten craft that will also help decorate your classroom.

Materials
construction paper
markers and crayons
glue
glitter
yarn
hole punch

left   right

Directions
On the chalkboard, draw a rectangle and write the words *left* and *right* inside it. (See the example.) Place your left hand over the word *left* on the chalkboard. Using your right hand, trace a mitten shape around your left hand. Emphasize the word *left*. Then have children trace around their left hand on the construction paper. Walk around the room to be sure everyone understands. Allow children to help each other with the tracing if necessary. Repeat this with the right hand. After both hands have been traced, instruct children to cut out their "mittens" and decorate them using markers, crayons and glitter. (It may be helpful to set up a glitter station to keep the sparkles confined to one area.) Display these winter works of art by punching a hole in the base of each mitten, connecting them with colorful yarn, and hanging them from the ceiling.

by Sheila M. Hausbeck

Frosty Finger Puppet Family

Materials

- scissors
- cotton balls
- black felt marker
- cellophane tape and dispenser
- craft glue and glue sticks
- shapes for cutting
- glitter, paint, stick-on eyes, sticky shapes (optional)

Let's Make It

1. Copy a snowperson shape for each child.
2. Have students cut out the snowperson shapes.
3. Children decorate their snowpersons, using the materials above.
4. Help the children make finger holders to fit their fingers.

Finger Puppet Stage

Materials

- shoe box
- craft knife (adult use only)
- acrylic paints

Let's Make It

1. Remove the lid and cut out the bottom of the shoe box, leaving a 2" (5 cm) border on the two short sides and one long side. The side with no border will be the bottom of the puppet stage.
2. Have children paint the puppet stage, let it dry, and put on a wintry performance for their friends.

by Robynne Eagan

Snowy Projects

Crystal Paintings

Children can see the magic of this painting transform as the paper dries. Measure equal amounts of Epsom salts and water. (Epsom salts can be bought at a local drugstore.) Heat the water until it boils; then gradually add the salt. Stir until the salt is dissolved (adult supervision is needed for this project). Give each child a small cup of this solution and a paintbrush. Have them paint on black construction paper. At first, the paper will just seem wet, but as the water evaporates, crystals will form on the page.

No-Melt Snowman

If you're in an area with no snow—don't despair. Make a class snowman with three white trash bags (the kind with draw strings) and leaves. Rake the leaves (a great gross motor activity) and stuff them into the trash bags (crumpled newspaper works, too). Tie the bag closed making use of the drawstrings. You might want to use the drawstrings to attach this snowman to a tree or pole so he doesn't topple over. Give your snowman a painted face and buttons. Add a hat and scarf. Voila, a homemade snowman that doesn't melt!

Pasta Flakes

Turn pasta shapes into ornate snowflakes. Arrange wagon wheels, bow ties and other dried pastas into different geometric patterns. It's best to work on a sheet of waxed paper or freezer paper. After your pattern is complete, gently apply glue to the edges and stick the pieces together. After the glue is completely dried, peel away the paper. Hang your snowflake with a piece of ribbon or yarn.

38
by Tania K. Cowling

A Pretty Snowflake

Did you ever think of using white coffee filters for paper snowflakes? It's fast, easy and inexpensive! Fold filter in half, half again and then once more. Cut designs along the edges. Open and have the children sign their names on each. Hang these snowflakes around the room. There will be so many varieties!

Note: Laminate these for durability. Also, you can alter the shape from a round snowflake to a star shape by cutting a wedge from the bottom edge.

Milk Jug Snowpeople

Collect three new milk jugs at the grocery store and turn them into cute snowpeople. If the jug you have is already white, you can start decorating. If not, paint the entire jug white. The milk jug lid can be painted another color. Add a pom-pom on top to make a hat. Glue on buttons, beads and googly eyes, and use fabric scraps for scarves. When dry, these cute snowpeople make seasonal decorations, or they can be filled with yummy treats!

Rice Snowman

On construction paper, draw the three circles to construct a snowman. Spread white school glue in the circle and pour on rice. Shake off the excess. Decorate with scraps of fabric. This art technique looks like a form of mosaic and shows texture.

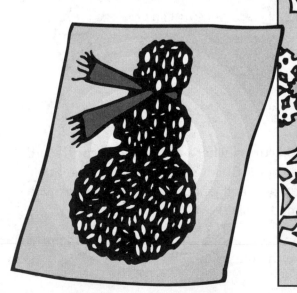

A Crafty Bookworm

Bookworm Materials

two 9" white or solid-colored paper plates
piece of construction paper, 6" x 18"
2' piece of cord
two 12" pipe cleaners
gummed circles of various colors and sizes
$3/4$" wide transparent tape
watercolor markers or crayons

Constructing a Bookworm

Make four loops of tape and place on the front side of one plate. Press the back of the other plate down on it.

Turn plates over. Draw a face or make one with colored stickers. Fold the construction paper in half, lengthwise. Fold, accordion style, into six sections. Trim one end section into a half egg shape.

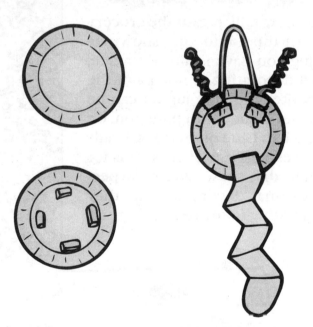

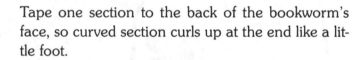

Tape one section to the back of the bookworm's face, so curved section curls up at the end like a little foot.

Turn ends of pipe cleaners down once or twice so there are no sharp points. Curl pipe cleaners around pencils. Remove pencils and stretch out pipe cleaners a little bit.

Tape an end of each pipe cleaner to the back of the bookworm's face. They should be approximately 2" from the top and 3" apart. Bend them so they look like feelers.

Tape the ends of the cord between the feelers, in back of the face. They should be close to the feelers and almost 3" from the top of the bookworm's head.

Hang the bookworms where the children can record book titles on them. Children can decorate the bookworms' bodies between and around the names with colored gummed circles.

When the bookworms are completed, hang them as mobiles or use them as puppets.

Have the children dance their bookworms to peppy music, bouncing them up and down, swaying them from side to side, and swinging them around.

by Mabel Duch

Children's Book Week Secret Hide-Away

Make a secret hiding spot for favorite books or other treasures.

Materials
- one book-sized box per student
- craft knives or scissors
- construction paper or tagboard
- paste
- paper
- writing instruments
- ruler

Let's Make It

1. Have each student bring in a book-sized box.

2. Assist students in cutting three sides of the box top about $\frac{1}{2}$" to 1" from the edge of the box to form a lid that can be opened and closed.

3. Students will cut white paper to fit along the right edge and sides of the box. Ensure that the paper completely covers the end of the box.

4. Children will measure and draw a series of straight lines along this paper to resemble the pages of a book.

5. The false page ends are pasted to the right edge of the box.

6. Students will then choose a color of construction paper or tagboard to cover the top of the box and wrap around the left side to cover the bottom of the box, resembling a book cover.

7. This cover is then decorated to look like a real book cover with a title, cover art, and author name. Students may invent a new book or try to re-create the cover of an existing book. The left edge should be made to look like the spine of the book.

8. The false cover is pasted to the bottom, back, and hidden lid of the box. The cover will hide the lid and the storage space within the box.

Book Week Booklets

Bring literature and art together during Book Week.

Materials
- story planning sheets
- paper
- construction paper or tagboard
- writing and drawing instruments

Let's Make It

1. Cut paper and construction paper into a variety of book shapes and sizes.

2. Provide students with a story planning sheet. This sheet is used to create a rough draft and plan of their story. After editing, a second sheet can be provided for a revised copy.

3. Students will take their revised copy to the Book Making Center to publish their work.

4. Allow students to choose their shape and size and assemble a book made up of the number of pages needed to tell their story.

5. Students will transfer their story text and illustrations to the booklet.

6. Create a "Book Shelf" bulletin board to display their efforts.

by Robynne Eagan

Tasty Tabletop Turkey

Materials

potato
kabob sticks
toothpicks
gumdrops
marshmallow
piece of licorice
scissors

Toothpicks

Directions

1. Firmly insert the ends of six toothpicks into the bottom of a potato, forming two side-by-side triangles. Turn the potato over. The toothpicks should provide a sturdy base for the turkey's feet.

2. Hold the potato with one hand and firmly insert three 5" kabob sticks across the top of the potato. Space sticks the length of the potato. Add four large gumdrops of various colors to each stick. Space gumdrops the length of each stick. The turkey now has feathers.

3. Insert the end of a toothpick into the middle front of the potato. Push a marshmallow onto the toothpick until it touches the potato. Then push the top of a 1" piece of licorice onto the toothpick until the licorice touches the marshmallow (licorice should hide the end of toothpick). The turkey now has a head and gobbler.

4. Cut pieces of gumdrop. Add these to the marshmallow to form the turkey's eyes and nose. Attach face with glue or toothpicks. The turkey is now complete. Place it on your table for a Thanksgiving centerpiece the whole family can enjoy.

Variations

Paint toothpicks and kabob sticks for colorful feathers and feet. Let sticks dry before inserting into potato. Raisins, m & m's®, and candy corn also make wonderful eyes and noses. Use your imagination on your turkey's face.

by Amanda Boor

Thanksgiving Craft Ideas

Nature Place Mat

Have children collect brightly colored fall leaves. Press them between paper towels for several days with something heavy stacked on top. When the leaves are flat, lay the pretty side on the sticky side of a piece of clear adhesive plastic, the size of a place mat. Lay a sheet of construction paper over the plastic. These place mats can be used in the classroom at snack time or sent home to be used when the family gathers for Thanksgiving dinner.

Gourd Pilgrims or Indians

Provide small, long-necked gourds for children to decorate and dress up. Use the large end of the gourd as the body and the small end as the head. The children can draw faces on the gourds, add yarn hair, hats, and paper or cloth clothing. To make the gourd stand, push the big end into clay.

Pinecone Turkeys

Gather pinecones on a nature walk. Provide colored feathers for children to glue to the large end of the pinecone. Pipe cleaners can be used to make the feet of the turkey. Cut the turkey's head out of construction paper and glue in place, at the small end of the pinecone.

Variation: Substitute large potatoes for pinecones.

Table Centerpiece

Have children gather dead and dry weeds and other things found in nature. Field corn or colored Indian corn are great additions. Slice an ear of corn into sections. Place the weeds into the soft center of the cut ears for place settings, or combine several for a centerpiece. Spray-paint the weeds for added color.

by Ann Curtis

Let's Celebrate Thanksgiving

Thanksgiving Table Decorations

Involve children in their family's celebration. Combine a seasonal craft as students practice skills of cutting and pasting. Make a place mat from a long sheet of seasonal-colored construction paper. Supply felt-tip markers for drawing turkeys or other November pictures. Laminate for durability.

For a napkin holder, cut an empty paper towel tube into 1½" sections. Glue a strip of felt in seasonal colors around each piece.

For napkins, purchase loosely woven fabric in brown or orange. Every 18" pull a thread to get a perfect square. Cut on this line. Show children how to fringe a 1" border around all four sides. One yard, 36" wide, makes four napkins.

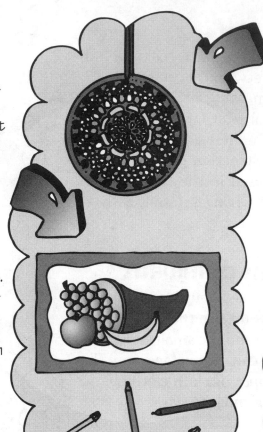

Thanksgiving Mosaic Design

Use the lid from a plastic container, such as sour cream or sandwich spread. Cut and glue a piece of brown felt to fit inside the lid. Make a design using dried corn, noodles and beans to form a mosaic design. Punch a hole near the top. Add a brown or orange ribbon or cord for hanging.

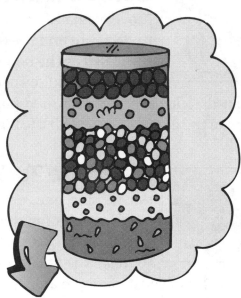

Pinecone Turkey

Collect pinecones of different sizes and shapes. If cones are wet, allow to dry. This will open the petals. Cut colored paper into feather shapes and glue between several petals. Make a head from brown paper. Color the wattle red.

Harvest Jar

Collect small narrow jars, such as olive jars, for each child. Purchase dried soup beans with a variety of colors and shapes. Fill one jar. Let the children guess how many beans are in the jar. Provide time for each student to layer colors and shapes in their own creation. These can be given to a special older friend before Thanksgiving.

by Carolyn Tomlin

Turkey Feast Name Card

Reproduce the patterns below on heavy paper. Color and cut out. Add child's name.
Wrap the turkey's body around a 5-oz. paper cup. Glue the tail to the back of the cup.

by Veronica Terrill

HANUKKAH
Do It Yourself

Dreidel Greeting Card

Materials:
- paper (construction, drawing or typing)
- crayons or markers
- scissors

What You Will Do:

1. Fold the paper in half.

2. Draw a dreidel on it, with one side of it touching the fold.

3. Cut out the dreidel through both pieces of paper. Do not cut through the fold.

4. Color or decorate the dreidel.

5. Write a message inside. Sign it.

6. Give it to a friend.

Countdown Calendar

This can be an individual project to make and take home, keeping one to display in the classroom.

Have the children cut two triangles out of construction paper, as well as eight strips of paper to make chains. The colors of Israel are blue and white.

Glue the two triangles together, one point up and one point down to form a Star of David. Use the strips to make circles, attaching each to form a chain. Assemble all these pieces together to form this countdown calendar.

Let the students take this calendar home, instructing them to remove one link each night of Hanukkah until the holiday is over.

by Tania Kourempis-Cowling

Foil Pictures

Cut two triangles from aluminum foil. Glue these onto a sheet of construction paper to form a Star of David. Prepare glue paint in cups by adding drops of food coloring to white glue. Let the children paint designs on the foil stars using small paintbrushes or cotton swabs. Every picture is creative and unique. Display these around the classroom.

Egg Carton Menorah

Materials:
- 1 egg carton (foam or cardboard)
- heavy-duty aluminum foil
- scissors
- thumbtacks
- white craft cement
- Hanukkah candles

What You Will Do:

1. Cut off the lid from the egg carton. Tear apart each cup.

2. Cut off the points from the tops of nine cups. This will leave a rounded top.

3. Cover the entire lid of the carton with foil. Cover each of the nine cups with foil.

4. Push a thumbtack up through the bottom of each foil-covered cup.

5. To make the shamash, get another cup from the egg carton. Do NOT cut off the points. Cut other points on the sides that are straight. Cover this cup with foil, molding the foil down between each point. Glue the bottom of this cup to the bottom of one of the other cups.

6. Glue each cup to the foil-lined lid. The shamash can be at one end, or in the middle, and will be higher.

7. Before putting the candles on the tacks, hold the bottom of each candle over a flame. This will soften the wax and keep it from cracking. The foil makes the menorah safe to use for lighting the candles.

How to Use the Menorah

1. The menorah will be used for eight nights to remember the miracle of the oil that burned for eight days.

2. Each night the shamash is lit and used to light the other candles. *Shamash* means "servant."

3. On the first night, one candle is lit. On the second night, two candles are lit. Each night another candle is added, until on the eighth night, all of the candles are lit.

4. The candles burn until they are gone. Do not blow them out.

5. Place the menorah in a safe place. A small table in front of a window lets others enjoy it.

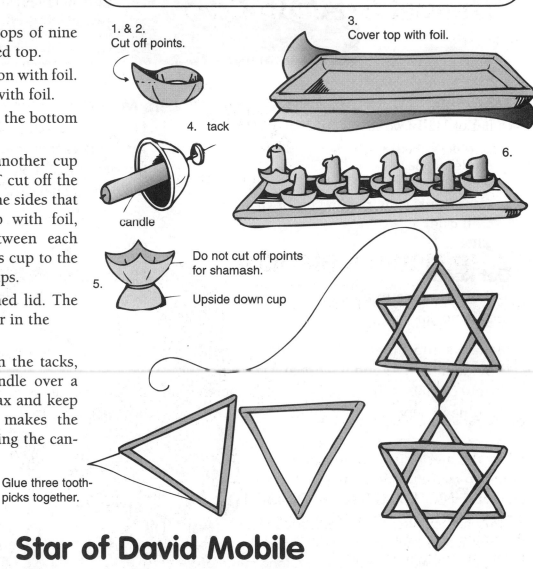

1. & 2. Cut off points.

3. Cover top with foil.

4. tack

candle

5. Do not cut off points for shamash.

Upside down cup

6.

Glue three toothpicks together.

Star of David Mobile

Materials:
- waxed paper
- toothpicks
- white glue
- thread

What You Will Do:

1. Spread out the waxed paper to work on.

2. Put glue on the tips of three toothpicks, and glue them together to form a triangle.

3. Make another triangle the same way.

4. Glue the second triangle upside down on top of the first one. Let dry.

5. Make as many stars as you want.

6. Loop the thread through the top point of one of the stars. Hang the second star from the first and so on until the mobile is as long as you want.

7. Instead of looping the stars together, you could hang each one (at different lengths) from a hanger or stick.

by Judy Wolfman

Simple Menorahs

Materials
- flat blocks of wood at least 1" high and 6" long
- modeling clay
- 9 crayons for each child
- small sturdy cups, muffin tins, or egg cups
- craft glue
- glitter

Get Ready
Talk to your group about Hanukkah and the menorah.

Make a sample menorah to guide children. Provide materials and a work space. Put a variety of glitters in the cups or containers. Put glue in separate containers.

Let's Make It
1. Have children choose a color of modeling clay, work it until it is soft, and then shape it over the top of the wood block until it is about 1" thick. Or mold individual candle holders as shown.

2. Instruct children to strip the wrappers from nine chosen crayons.

3. Have children dip the tops of the crayons in a pot of glue, one at a time, and then dip the tips in cups of glitter. After the crayons have their glitter "flame" ready, have children push the crayons into the modeling clay base.

4. When all crayons are in place, children can marvel at their nine candles shining bright!

by Robynne Eagan

Playdough Menorah
Provide children with playdough and purchased birthday candles. They can make a base with the playdough rolled into a long menorah. Children place a larger candle in the center for a shammash and then four small candles on each side to complete the menorah. Make sure that there is no way the children can light the candles.

by Ann Curtis

STAR OF DAVID

Place a sheet of waxed paper over the top of the pattern. Fill the outlined area with white glue and sprinkle with glitter as illustrated. Let dry completely (about 5-7 days) and carefully peel from waxed paper. Attach string to hang.

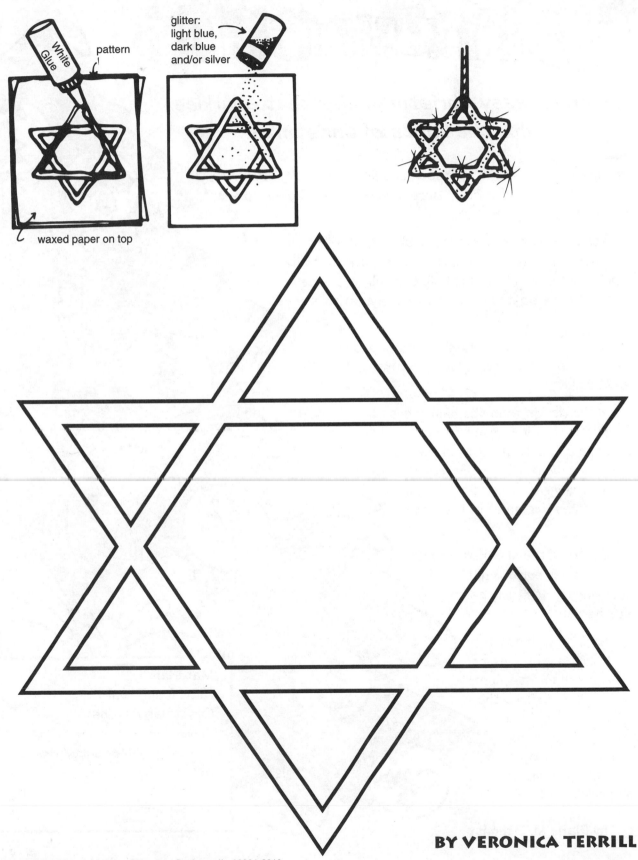

BY VERONICA TERRILL

Snowball Ornaments

A quick, easy Christmas idea that sparkles with the lights of Christmas!

Directions

Cut a pipe cleaner into fourths and push one piece into a Styrofoam™ ball about 1½". Pull it out and put a drop of glue in the hole, then push the pipe cleaner back into the hole.

Cut out two to three designs from the napkins that will fit on the ball. The designs don't have to be cut perfectly because the white part of the napkin will blend in with the ball. Carefully separate the layers of the napkin so there is only one layer with the design.

Mix equal amounts of water and glue in a cup. Use the paintbrush to spread the glue mixture onto the Styrofoam™ ball.

Gently place the design from the napkin onto the ball, tapping it down into the glue. Start from the middle and work out to the edges to avoid wrinkles. More glue mixture can be added if needed. Be sure the first design is stuck to the ball, then add the other design(s) in the same manner.

Liberally add more of the glue mixture with the paintbrush, then sprinkle glitter all over the ornament. Hang the ball to let the glue harden.

When the glue is dry, ribbon can be added at the base of the pipe cleaner. These ornaments sparkle and glitter as they reflect the lights of the tree. The ornament is ready to be hung on the Christmas tree or to be wrapped as a gift for someone special.

by Diana M. Schmitt

Materials
Styrofoam™ ball
Christmas napkins
white glue
one-sided glitter (it looks clear to white)
ribbon
pipe cleaner
paintbrush

Multicultural Holiday Banners
Reusing Last Year's Christmas Cards

Materials

- thin dowel rod (about 10" long)
- piece of felt about 6" x 8"
- fabric pieces
- glue
- Christmas cards

Finally, here's something to do with last year's Christmas cards! Banners are becoming more and more popular everywhere you turn. Your students are all familiar with the many sizes and styles of banners that are available. You can make multicultural banners as a holiday project right in your own classroom.

Have students select a cultural theme for their banner. Make a list on the board: Kwanzaa, Hanukkah, St. Lucia's Day, Mexico, Hawaiian Joyeaux Noel and so on. On paper, sketch an idea for the banner. Encourage your students to use a symbol for their theme, such as a menorah, palm tree or a crown of candles.

Using the Christmas cards and fabric pieces, begin to cut and assemble the pattern for your banner. Use words and pictures from the cards. When your cultural picture is complete, be ready to glue it to your piece of felt. First fold over the top of the felt to make a pocket for the dowel rod, and secure it in place using glue. When the glue has dried completely, slide the dowel rod through. Now glue your cultural theme onto the felt to complete your banner. This activity is an ideal project for cooperative learning groups. Assign a leader for each group and allow the students to brainstorm before beginning. Make it a classroom contest. Hang the completed projects on a wall using pushpins under the dowel rods. You may also hang the banners with ribbon or string.

by Jo Jo Cavalline and Jo Anne O'Donnell

Winter White Decorations

Materials

1 cup (250 ml) cornstarch
2 cups (500 ml) baking soda
1/4 cup (63 ml) water
rolling pin
waxed paper
straws for making holes
cookie cutters

Let's Make It

1. Stir ingredients together in a saucepan and cook over medium heat. Stir constantly until the mixture thickens to a doughy consistency.

2. Turn the dough out onto a board or other work surface and let it stand until cool enough to handle.

3. Have children lightly dust their hands and work surface with cornstarch.

4. Children will knead the warm dough for a minute or two, and then leave the dough covered with a damp cloth until cool.

5. Have children dust a rolling pin with cornstarch and roll their dough to exactly 1/8" (2.5 mm) thick.

6. Children will lightly dust a cookie cutter with cornstarch and cut out shapes.

7. A small straw can be pressed into the shape to form a hole where ribbon can be threaded when the decoration dries.

8. Use a spatula to move decorations to a flat surface covered with wax paper.

9. Turn decorations every two hours to ensure proper drying.

10. When the decoration has dried, a length of white ribbon can be threaded through the hole and tied at the ends for hanging.

Tips

- Smaller cookie cutters work best with this clay.

- Children should handle these decorations carefully as they are fragile once dry.

- Cooled dough can be sealed in a plastic container and kept for several weeks unrefrigerated or used right away. Knead the dough before using, and add a few drops of water if the dough is too dry or a pinch of cornstarch if it becomes sticky.

52

by Robynne Eagan

SUPER SANTAS

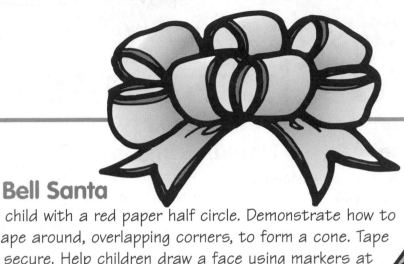

Bell Santa

Provide each child with a red paper half circle. Demonstrate how to bend this shape around, overlapping corners, to form a cone. Tape or staple to secure. Help children draw a face using markers at the pointed end of the cone, then glue cotton around the face. Instruct children to slide one end of a pipe cleaner through the slot on a jingle bell and twist the pipe cleaner to hold the bell securely. Insert the opposite end of the pipe cleaner up into the cone and out through the top. Glue the pipe cleaner to the cone on the top; then add a cotton ball to form a pom-pom for the pointed hat. Bend the pipe cleaner into a handle/hanger.

Egg Carton Santa

Create Santa ornaments from egg carton cups. Have children glue one end of a piece of red tissue paper around the opening of their cups. Show them how to gather the opposite end of the tissue paper together and secure it with tape to form a hat shape. Let them add facial features to the front of the cup using markers. Add cotton for whiskers and hair around Santa's face, as well as for a hatband and pom-pom. Use a tapestry needle to insert a length of yarn, knotted at the bottom, through the cup. Tie the yarn into a loop for hanging and secure the bottom knot with glue.

by Marie E. Cecchini

7 ways to recycle old Christmas cards

Christmas Card Frames

Materials:
lightweight cardboard (you could use a cereal box), Christmas cards, white glue, a glue stick and a photograph (3½" x 5" or 4" x 6" works best)

Directions:
Cut the cards into triangles. Cut the cardboard into rectangles about 1" larger than the photo you are using. Have children glue the photo to the center of the cardboard, using a glue stick. At this point, it is helpful to cover the center of the photo with a Post-it™. This protects the photo from glue.

Next, glue the Christmas card triangles all around the photo. Place the flat edge of the triangles against the photo, letting the points stick out. Putting three or four layers of triangles on the frame will make it sturdier and more attractive.

Christmas Napkin Rings

Materials:
cardboard tube from paper towels, Christmas wrapping paper, old Christmas cards

Directions:
Cut the cardboard tube into rings that are about 1¼" wide. Cover the rings with Christmas wrapping paper. Cut out seasonal pictures from old Christmas cards. Glue a picture onto each covered ring.

At Christmas dinner, slip napkins into the napkin rings and put one at each place setting.

by D.A. Woodliff

Collage Tree

This is another great way to use old Christmas cards. Cut the cards into small triangles using the method shown. Don't worry about being exact! Duplicate a simple tree outline for each child. Children then glue triangles on the outline to create a collage tree.

Christmas Weaving

This project provides good exercise for little hands with pretty results. Trim two cards so they are the same size. Cut one into strips and the other into a mat as shown.

by Mary Maurer

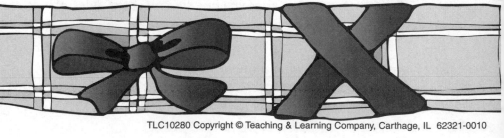

Christmas Border

Christmas cards can easily become a decorative accessory in your classroom. One idea is to use old cards to dress up your holiday bulletin board.

Use large cards and trim them so they are all the same size. Then cut the cards as shown to form two triangles.

To make a border, you'll need long strips of paper or poster board. Typing paper or copy paper can be used by cutting each sheet in half horizontally and gluing the sheets together to make one long strip. Assemble cards as shown, and glue on the paper strip for stability. Staple or tack the border to your bulletin board.

Cozy Quilt Bulletin Board

Recycle Christmas cards into an old-fashioned bulletin board. Although you can make this bulletin board yourself, you'll have much more fun letting your students make the squares and assemble the "quilt."

To begin, cut 7" squares of green and red construction paper. Then cut old Christmas cards into triangles.

Glue card triangles to construction paper to form a "quilt square." Assemble squares on bulletin board as shown.

Peek-a-Boo Plates

Materials:

white glue, glitter or poster paint, two paper plates, Christmas card, pipe cleaner or yarn, hole punch, scissors

Directions:

Cut Christmas card picture to fit center of plate. "Scene" cards work best. Card should be big enough to cover most of the center portion of the plate.

Cut Christmas tree, ornament, star or snowman pattern from center of second plate.

Lightly paint reverse side of cut plate, or coat with glue and sprinkle with glitter. Let dry.

Glue cut plate to card plate, centering opening over scene or design on card. Punch hole and use pipe cleaner or yarn to hang.

by Mary Maurer

Cone Christmas Tree

Advance Preparation: Prepare green paper circles—8", 10", or 12" diameter. Put glitter in saltshakers so that it is easy to use.

Get

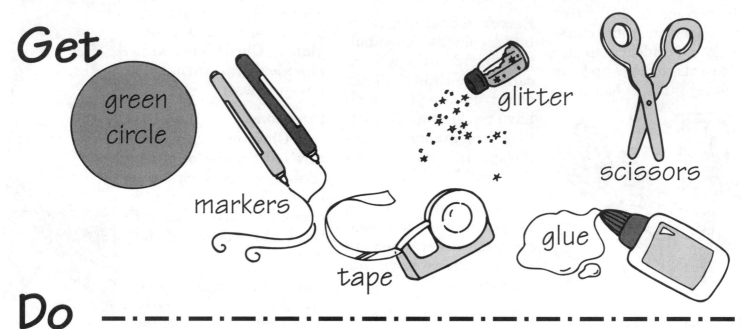

green circle

markers

glitter

scissors

tape

glue

Do

1. Cut.

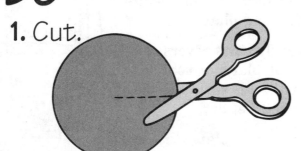

2. Decorate.

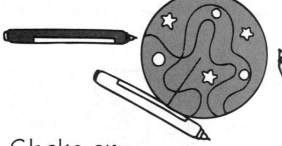

3. Dab on glue.

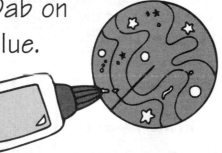

4. Shake on glitter.

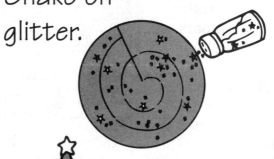

5. Roll and tape.

Cone Christmas Trees

by Carol Ann Bloom

The Art of Giving

Celebrate the magic of the season with great gift-giving projects.

Bath Scents

Supplies
baking soda, essential oil or perfume, food coloring, envelopes, markers, plastic cups, plastic spoons, measuring cup

Instructions
1. Have each child measure $1/4$ c. baking soda into a plastic cup. Help the children add a few drops of both essential oil or perfume and food coloring to the baking soda. Have the children mix the ingredients thoroughly. Set the mixtures aside.

2. Let each child decorate an envelope with markers. Have the students spoon their scented bath salts from the cups into the envelopes; then seal the envelopes.

Holiday Napkin Holder

Supplies
pasta boxes, cardboard, yellow construction paper, star pattern, tape, glue, scissors, ruler

Instructions
1. Have the children measure 2" up from the bottom of their boxes and draw a line. Cut around the box on this line. Set the top of the box aside. Cover the 2" section with yellow construction paper. Tape the paper in place to secure.

2. Have the children use the star pattern to trace and cut two yellow paper stars and two cardboard stars (use the cardboard from the top portion of the box). Glue the yellow paper stars to the cardboard ones.

3. Glue one star to each long side of the yellow box bottom to make a napkin holder. Variation: Use as a paper holder on a desktop.

pattern

by Marie E. Cecchini   **57**

Bag Wrap

Supplies

paper lunch bags, cardboard, yellow paper, scissors, glue, tape, ruler, pencil, stapler

Instructions

1. Have the children measure and mark a line 4" from the top of their bag. Cut on this line to remove the bag top. Discard the top.

2. Open the bottom section of the bag. Trace the bottom of the bag on cardboard. Cut out this cardboard rectangle and place it in the bottom of the bag.

3. Help the children fold over the top edges of their bag to make a flap all the way around. Cut strips of yellow paper and glue the strips to the flap on all four sides.

4. Let the children draw and cut star shapes from the yellow paper. Glue these star decorations to the sides of the bags.

5. Cut a cardboard strip handle for each bag. Let the children wrap their handles in yellow paper, taping the paper to secure. Staple the ends of the handle to the sides of the bag.

6. Stuff tissue paper into each bag. Place a gift in the tissue paper.

Candle Jar

Supplies

small glass jars (such as baby food), clear nail polish, glitter, votive candles

Instructions

1. Have the children brush clear nail polish around the neck of their jar; then sprinkle the wet nail polish with glitter.

2. Let the children brush clear nail polish designs around their jars, working one section at a time, and sprinkle these wet designs with glitter.

3. Allow the polish to dry. Set a votive candle into each jar.

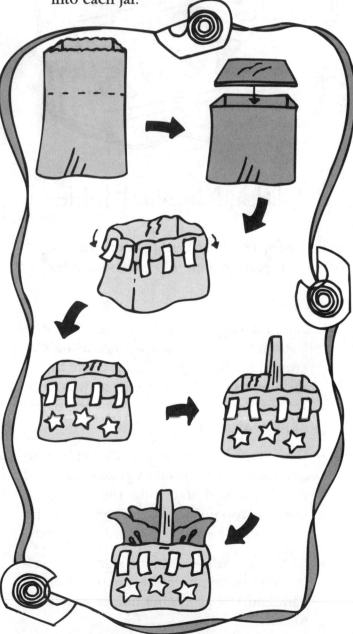

Christmas Tree
Wind Sock

1. Paint paper snow cone cup green.

2. Sprinkle with glue and glitter. Add sequins beads, and so on.

3. Attach a jingle bell to a piece of ribbon or yarn.

Tie a knot 1$\frac{1}{2}$" from the bell. Pull through a hole in the top.

4. Tape or glue 1" x 10" or 12" pieces of red and white crepe paper to the inside of the cone as shown.

by Veronica Terrill

Gingerbread People Holiday Garland

Stop!

*Don't throw away the cardboard backs
of your empty notebooks.
Recycle them without even sorting them into
the correct bin.
Use the cardboard to create holiday gingerbread
people garland in three easy steps.*

Materials

notebook backs or lightweight cardboard
curly ribbon or yarn—red or green
ruler
markers
scissors
pencil
paper punch
gingerbread man and woman patterns (page 61)

Directions

Step 1: Trace the gingerbread man and woman patterns onto the cardboard. You should be able to fit three on each piece of cardboard. Cut out the shapes.
Note: Twelve men make a nice length of garland.

Step 2: Gingerbread cookies are frosted, so use markers to "ice" one side of the gingerbread men and women. You can make them identical, use red and green for a holiday theme, or decorate each one differently.

Step 3: After all your gingerbread people have been decorated, punch a hole in the center of each hat. Cut two pieces of ribbon 42" long. From the end of the ribbon, measure 6". Mark the measurement on the ribbon with your pencil. Loop the ribbon through the punched hole, move the gingerbread person to the pencil mark, and tie a knot. With your ruler measure out another 6", make a mark, and tie the next gingerbread person to the marked spot on the ribbon. Repeat this until all the gingerbread men and women are secured to the ribbon.
Note: Cutting two pieces of ribbon makes it easier to work with. You can tie the end of the ribbon together to make the 12 gingerbread people garland.

Now that you are finished, it's time to display your recycled creation. It can be strung around the Christmas tree, draped across the fireplace mantel, or hung around a door or window frame. Enjoy!

by Rose Ross Zediker

Holiday Gifts

Invite your children to practice the art of giving with the following gift-making activities.

Spice Sachet

Supplies

envelopes, talcum powder (unscented, if possible), salt, cinnamon, nutmeg, allspice, cloves, vanilla extract, markers, tape, plastic cups, measuring spoons, plastic spoons

Instructions

1. Let the children measure and mix 2 tsp. talcum, 2 tsp. salt, and 1 tsp. each of the dry ingredients into individual plastic cups. Help them to add a few drops of vanilla extract to each cup. Have them stir their mixtures until no wet spots remain. Set the cups aside.

2. Let the children decorate the envelopes with markers.

3. Help the children spoon the mixture from their cups into their envelopes. Let them seal the envelopes. Tape to further secure, if desired.

Rope Soap

Supplies

soap pieces, cornmeal, vegetable oil, peppermint extract, water, green food coloring, string, blender, mixing bowl, measuring cup, measuring spoons

Instructions

1. Collect soap pieces and/or small hand soaps. Have the children place 1 c. soap pieces and 1 c. cornmeal into a blender. Pulverize the mixture to a coarse powder. Pour the powder into a bowl.

2. Help the children measure and add 4 tablespoons of vegetable oil, a few drops of peppermint extract, 2 tablespoons of warm water, and a few drops of green food coloring to the powder. Let the children mix and mash the ingredients together with their hands; then shape the mixture around the end of a loop of string. Allow the soap to dry before using.

Note: This recipe makes enough for two soaps.

by Marie E. Cecchini

Ribbon Dispenser

Supplies

plastic icing containers, holiday stickers, scissors or a sharp knife (for adult use)

Instructions

1. Use the scissors or knife to cut an X in the lid of each icing container.

2. Have the children decorate their containers with holiday stickers.

3. To use the dispenser, place ribbon into the container, thread the end of the ribbon up through the X-shaped slit; then snap the lid onto the container. **Variations:** 1) Use the dispenser for string. 2) Make a long slit in the top and use to dispense stickers or postage stamps.

Corn Print Wrap

Supplies

ears of corn, newsprint, foam trays, various colors of liquid tempera paint, newspaper

Instructions

1. Cover the working surface with newspaper. Spread the paint in the foam trays, one tray per color.

2. Have the children roll the ears of corn in the paint; then across a piece of newsprint.

3. Allow the paint to dry; then let the children use the paper to wrap the gifts they made.

Note: Use this project to challenge the children to copy color patterns provided by you. Also have them note any color changes created by mixing colors.

Pattern

Star Tags

Supplies

star pattern, yellow paper, gold glitter, yellow yarn, hole punch, glue, markers, scissors

Instructions

1. Trace and cut out the star pattern above from cardboard. Have the children use the cardboard patterns to make yellow paper stars. Let them edge the stars with a line of glue and sprinkle the glue with gold glitter. Allow the glue to dry.

2. Help the children punch holes at the top of their stars, thread the holes with lengths of yellow yarn, and knot the yarn ends.

3. Help the children write on their tags (to/from, Happy Holidays, and so on.)

You-Make-'Em Christmas Crafts

Deer or Reindeer Treats

Materials
brown paper lunch bag
shredded wheat
crayons, markers, or colored paper
stapler
paper tags

Let's Make It
1. Cut out the middle portion of the top two-thirds of the bag, leaving antler shapes on either side of the bag.

2. Have children make a deer face on the bag by adding eyes and a nose. A round red sticker may be used in place of Rudolph's nose or a black sticker for other deer or reindeer.

3. Have students mix up their own deer treats by adding one cup of various foods like wheat, oatmeal, etc.

4. Staple the bag closed, attaching a tag that reads *Deer treats made by* _____. Each child takes a bag home and sprinkles the treats in the yard for the reindeer.

Helping Hands Christmas Tree

Materials
green construction paper
paste
round, pre-pasted stickers
pencil
scissors

Let's Make It
1. Help children each trace their hands on the construction paper.

2. Help children cut out the hand shapes and and label each with their names.

3. Using scissors, gently curl the fingers of the hand cut out.

4. Allow children to decorate the hands using the sticky shapes provided.

5. Combine the hands on a bulletin board or classroom door to form a Helping Hands Christmas Tree.

by Robynne Eagan

Roll a Candle

This easy-to-make gift is sure to brighten the holiday season for parents, grandparents, and friends. The candles can be used to brighten Thanksgiving, Christmas, Kwanzaa, or Hanukkah.

Materials

sheets of beeswax
candlewick
scissors
fine glitter

Let's Make It

1. Pre-cut beeswax sheets into squares the size you desire.

2. Help students press the wick along one edge of a sheet. Trim the wick, leaving about 1/4" at the top.

3. Show children how to roll the beeswax evenly and slowly to hide the wick inside and form a candle. Candles can be warmed in children's hands and reformed somewhat if necessary.

4. Finished candles can be rolled in a tray of glitter.

5. Have children wrap finished candles in tissue paper and attach a gift tag.

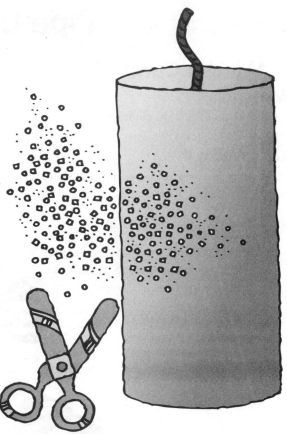

Mini Cone Christmas Trees

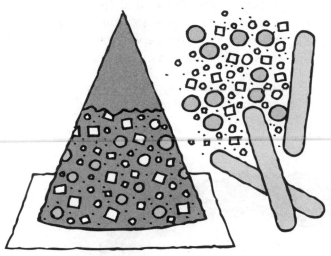

Materials

royal icing (See recipe below.)
mini cones (for ice cream)
pastry bags and decorating tips
craft sticks
cookie decorations: colored sprinkles, silver balls, small candies

Recipe for Royal Icing

3 egg whites
1/2 tsp. (2 ml) cream of tartar
pinch of salt
1 lb. (500 g) confectioner's sugar

1. Beat the egg whites, cream of tartar, and salt until soft peaks form.

2. Cover the mixture with a damp cloth until needed.

Let's Make It

1. Have children dip the bottom of the cone in the icing, and then place upside down on a doily on a square or circle of cardboard.

2. Children can coat the cone with icing, and then sprinkle and press decorations on the Christmas tree while icing is still damp. Cover with a damp cloth if necessary to dampen.

3. Colored or white frosting may be squeezed over the creation using the pastry bag and tip. Let dry.

4. Place the festive trees around the classroom for decorations, or have children take them home.

5. Children can eat these creations when they have finished admiring them.

Pipe Cleaner Creations

Wind a Candy Cane

Materials

red and white pipe cleaners

Let's Make It

1. Join one end of a red pipe cleaner to one end of a white pipe cleaner.

2. Fold the pipe cleaners at the joint.

3. Wind the red and white together, and then shape the top to form a simple candy cane.

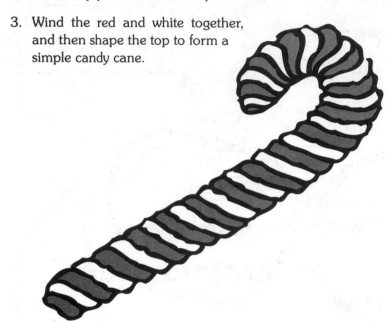

Crafty Christmas Tree

Materials

fluffy green pipe cleaner
Christmas tree cookie cutter
red construction paper
green spinach-colored pasta or green sequins
high-quality craft paste and paste brush
large tray or bin
gold or silver pipe cleaner

Let's Make It

1. Help children shape a pipe cleaner to form a Christmas tree. This can be done by shaping it free hand of around a template or cookie cutter. Two pipe cleaners may be joined together if necessary.

2. Children will paste the frame to the red construction paper and let dry.

3. Put uncooked spinach pasta in a bag and crush.

4. Have the children paint paste inside the Christmas tree shape, and then sprinkle the crushed pasta or green sequins over the glue and gently shake the paper back and forth. The excess can be poured onto a tray.

5. Gold pipe cleaners can be shaped to form a Christmas star and garlands and added to complete the effect.

Twist a Wreath

Materials

green pipe cleaners
green, red, and gold beads

Let's Make It

1. Have children thread green beads, and a few red, white, or gold beads, onto pipe cleaners.

2. When the length of the pipe cleaner is filled with beads, children can twist the ends together to form a Christmas wreath.

3. A second green pipe cleaner can be threaded around and between the beads to create a bushier effect.

First Fruits of Kwanzaa Bowl

Reproduce the patterns below. Color and cut out. Glue the bowl, as illustrated, to red, green, or black construction paper to form a pocket. Place the fruit in the pocket as you learn the seven principles of Kwanzaa.

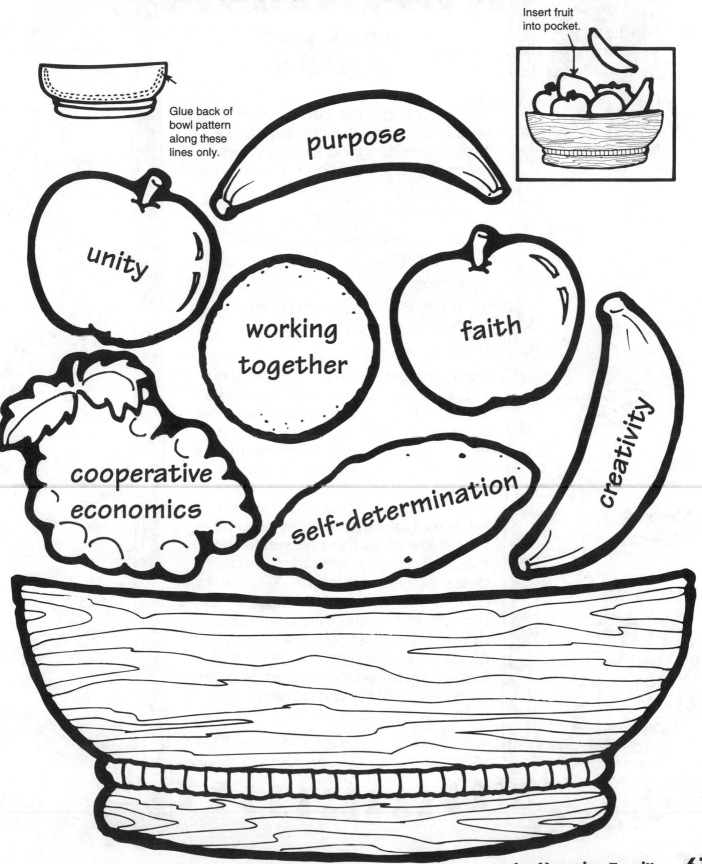

Glue back of bowl pattern along these lines only.

Insert fruit into pocket.

purpose

unity

working together

faith

creativity

cooperative economics

self-determination

KWANZAA VEST

While holding a Kwanzaa celebration in your class, allow the children to dress in their newly designed Kwanzaa vests. It is easy to make and here is what you need:

- brown grocery bag
- black, red, green, and yellow paint
- scissors
- black, red, green, and yellow yarn (optional)
- glue

Open the bag up fully. If there is an imprint on it, you may wish to turn it inside out when forming the vest. First cut a slit straight up the front of the vest. Then cut a round section for the neck. Place the bag around the child's shoulders and find the correct spot for the armholes. Cut two armholes so that the child can slip on the vest. Now allow the children to show their individuality and creativity by designing the vest for the Kwanzaa holiday. Make the paints and paintbrushes available to them. They can make stripes or designs using the Kwanzaa colors. If yarn is available, they can fringe the bottom of the vest by gluing yarn pieces of various colors to the hem.

by Jo Jo Cavalline and
Jo Anne O'Donnell

LET'S CELEBRATE KWANZAA!

MAKE KWANZAA DRUMS

Cover large coffee cans or oatmeal boxes with off-white or beige paper. Using red, green, and black paper, decorate the drums with geometric or stylized designs. Cut some of the paper into strips 3/4" and 1 1/2" wide, or use colored adhesive-backed plastic tape to create designs.

KWANZAA CANDLES

Materials

white paper
yellow paint in small containers
    with eyedroppers
drinking straws
thin black marker and crayons

Directions

1. Children draw seven candles with crayons.

2. Children place a drop of yellow paint on their paper above each candle and blow it around with a straw to form a flame. Leave flat to dry.

3. When the paint is dry, children print one principle in each flame.

SEVEN PRINCIPLES OF KWANZAA

UNITY
SELF-DETERMINATION
WORKING TOGETHER
SHARING
PURPOSE
CREATIVITY
FAITH

Over the holidays, seven candles are lit to represent these guiding principles.

BY MABEL DUCH

Happy New Year Crafts

Simple Bells

Materials
small jingle bells
gold and silver pipe cleaners

Let's Make It
1. Supply the materials and let children create.
2. Shakers, bracelets, and anklets can be made by threading the bells onto the wires and twisting the ends together.

Glitzy Shaker

Materials
clear plastic containers (water bottles work well)
brightly colored beans, beads, buttons, and marbles
confetti or large glitter flakes
red electrical tape

Let's Make It
1. Fill a bottle about half full with your choice of materials.
2. Fasten the cap tightly and wrap with electrical tape.
3. Shake in the new millennium.

Drum Up Some Enthusiasm

Materials
tin or cardboard round containers with plastic lids
colored pencils or dowel rods about ¼" (.6 cm) in diameter
construction paper or adhesive vinyl
markers, paint or stickers
masking tape

Let's Make It
1. Decorate the exterior of the container with construction paper or adhesive vinyl, stickers and paint or markers.
2. Replace the cover of the container.
3. Make drumsticks by wrapping the ends of colored pencils or dowels with masking tape until you have a ball on the end.

by Robynne Eagan

Tambourine Shaker

Materials

two aluminum pie plates
masking tape
rice or beans

Let's Make It

1. Place one pie plate faceup on the work surface.
2. Fill the plate half full of rice or beans.
3. Place the second pie plate upside down on top of the first so that the edges of the pie plates meet.
4. Help the children run tape around the edge where the two plates meet. Ensure that the tape is securely fastened. You may need to run a second band around the edge just to be sure.
5. Decorate the pie plate with stickers and shake it up!

Sponge On!

Familiarize students with the number of the new year while they have some crafty fun.

Materials

sponge shapes: for each number of the new year
bowl with clean water
paint tray (plastic plates, bowls, or pie plates)
acrylic paints
blotting pad (absorbent paper or cloth)
white art paper
masking tape

Let's Make It

1. Talk about the "new" year, has just arrived. Look at the number of the year together. What numerals do they see?
2. Prepare the materials before children arrive. Tape the art paper to a table. Fill bowls with only a little paint so children won't be able to get too much paint on their sponges.
3. Have children wet the sponges and wring them out.
4. Show children how to dip one side of the sponge gently into the paint bowl. Advise them not to soak up too much paint or it will make blotches on their paper.
5. Have children dab the sponge on the blotting pad until it leaves an image of the number. Children can then make the number on their art page.

Make a New Year Fortune-Teller

Predict the future with this kid-appealing fortune-teller of sorts.
All you need is a square piece of paper and a pencil.

Let's Make It

1. Fold the paper diagonally in half both ways and mark the center point with a dot.

2. Fold the corners towards the center so the points meet at the center dot. This will form a small square.

3. Flip the square over and fold the corners to the center once again to make an even smaller square.

4. Flip the square over again and print a timely word on each square pocket. Fold each of the triangles out. Write predictions on each side of the triangles—two for each fold.

5. Flip the square over again and print a numeral on each small triangle. Fold the fortune corners back down to hide the secrets within.

6. Gently bring the four corner points toward the center. Pull the center point down while pushing your thumb and forefingers into the four paper pockets on the outside and prepare to predict!

7. Ask participants to choose one of the four visible words. Spell the word while moving your fingers to flip the pockets in and out.

8. The participant then chooses one of the visible numbers. Flip your fingers back and forth again, counting out the chosen number and revealing more number selections.

9. Have the participant select another number. Raise that numbered triangle and reveal the New Year's prediction beneath.

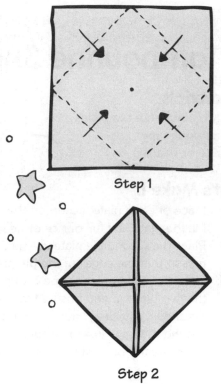

Step 1

Step 2

Step 3

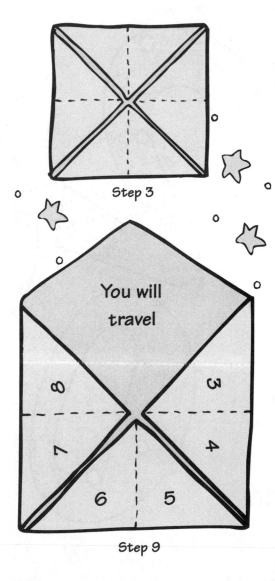

You will travel

Step 9

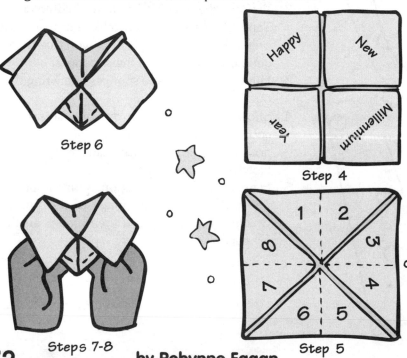

Step 6

Steps 7-8

Step 4

Step 5

by Robynne Eagan

Happy New Year!

Celebration Hats

Children will enjoy beginning a New Year's celebration by creating party hats. You will need ready-made party hats in assorted colors, an assortment of colored ribbons cut in 6" lengths, a pattern of each number needed to write out the year, glue, glitter sequins, and colored construction paper.

Let each child choose a party hat. Each child will trace the numbers on colored construction paper. Next, cut out the numerals. Glue the number "2" on the front of the hat. Glue the three other numbers on the remaining three sides of the party hat.

Children may decorate their party hats further by adding glitter and sequins to the hat and numerals. Attach several colored ribbons to the crown of the hat. When completed, children can wear their hats for the New Year's festivities. (For activities using the actual year, insert the current year.)

by Susan Jordan

Memory Pillow

Part of bringing in any new year is remembering experiences and people from the last year. Help your child make those memories more concrete by making a memory pillow. For the pillow cover, choose a pillowcase from a special sleepover, vacation or other occasion or a favorite article of clothing your child has outgrown. Let your child use fabric paint or permanent markers to decorate this pillow cover with pictorial reminders of events or people. If you use a favorite shirt, stitch the sleeves and neckline closed. Sleeves may also be cut off before decorating. Have your child stuff this special pillowcase or favorite article of clothing with cotton batting. Stitch the opening closed to complete the pillow and preserve the memories.

by Marie Cecchini

Music Makers

Make several traditional musical instruments and try two new ones, to celebrate February, Music Month.

Paper Plate Tambourine

Put a handful of dried beans, buttons, or pebbles between two paper plates or aluminum pie pans. Staple the edges. The plates can be decorated with markers. Lace or ribbons can be laced through holes placed around the edges of the tambourine.

Shoe Box Guitar

Place a number of large rubber bands around an open shoe box or shoe box lid. Try different thicknesses of rubber bands for different sounds. The shoe box and lid can be painted or covered with paper before rubber bands are added. Use plastic tab fasteners (from bread bags) as guitar picks.

Ankle/Wrist Bells

Thread jingle bells on yarn to tie on wrists and ankles. Make music when you move and walk.

Cardboard Tube Flute

Place a row of holes in the top of a paper towel tube. Cover one end with waxed paper and secure the paper with a rubber band. The child hums in the open end and uses the fingers on the flute holes. The tube can be colored with markers or decorated with stickers.

Can Drum

Tape the plastic lids on coffee cans and peanut cans for safety purposes. Use pencils, chopsticks, or wooden craft sticks as drumsticks. Wrap a rubber band several times around one end of a pencil to make a drumstick with a different sound. Cut wallpaper or gift wrap to tape around can drums. Attach a zigzag of yarn with glue to complete the drum.

Buzzing Button

Thread a 36" piece of string through both holes of a large two-hole button. Tie the ends of the string together. Hold a loop of the string in each hand with the button in the middle. Keep one hand still and rotate the other hand to wind the string tightly. Pull both loops to tighten the string and spin the button. Rewind the button by moving both hands closer together. Slowly move hands closer together and apart to keep the button spinning. Listen to the buzzing music.

Air Whistler

Cut a 4" x 6" piece of cardboard. Remove the center of the cardboard leaving a 1" border on the long side and a 3/4" border on the short side. Place a hole in the center of one of the 6" sides and tie a 2" string through the hole. Slide four rubber bands loosely around the 6" sides of the cardboard. Hold the end of the string and whirl the cardboard over the head in a circle. Listen as the air whistler makes its music.

by Carol Ann Bloom

Chinese New Year Fun

With the new moon between January 21 and February 19 comes the first day of the lunar calendar and the celebration of the Chinese New Year.

Chinese New Year Dragon

Materials

red, black, and green plasticine
clay modeling tools (improvise with pencils, craft sticks, scissors, pegs, fork, garlic press, and small rolling pin)
pictures or models of dragons

Let's Make It

1. Provide the materials and allow children full exploration of this three-dimensional media.

2. Praise all artistic efforts and provide freedom for variations of this complicated creature.

Try This

Display the dragons on a bed of crepe paper. Attach paper tags to each creation for easy identification.

by Robynne Eagan

Lanterns

On the fifteenth (last) day of the New Year festival, family members carry a lighted lantern in a parade. The people march alongside friends in a silk and bamboo-covered dragon costume. Make lanterns to decorate the classroom. Fold a 9$\frac{1}{2}$" x 11" piece of construction paper in half lengthwise. Draw a line across the paper 1" from the top. Tell the children to cut slits about 1" apart from the fold up to the line. Unfold; curve the lantern around and staple. Attach a paper handle.

Paper Fans

Cut circles (8" diameter) from poster board. Also, clip small squares of colorful tissue paper. Brush the entire circle with white glue; then place the tissue squares on, overlapping each piece. Make a handle by gluing on two tongue depressors, inserting the circle in between while the glue is wet. It would look nice to decorate both sides of the fan.

by Tania K. Cowling

Freedom Stand-Up

Honor Martin Luther King, Jr. with this special craft which students can take home as a reminder of what King stood for.

Materials

4½" x 10" piece of heavy art paper
6" x 11" piece of poster board (light color)
scissors
pencil
glue
colored markers or crayons
star stickers

Directions

1. Accordion fold the 4½" x 10" piece of paper into five sections.
2. Use the pencil to draw the outlines of a person with arms stretched out to either side on the folded paper.
3. Cut out the figure. Do not cut across the folds where the arms are.
4. Unfold the paper for a line of five identical people figures holding hands.
5. Color each figure a different color to represent different races of people.
6. Fold the 6" x 11" poster board in half lengthwise so it stands up.
7. Use a marker to print across the bottom of the poster board stand-up *One nation under God with liberty and justice for all*. (Be sure to underline the word <u>all</u>.)
8. Glue the connected people figures across the top of the stand-up piece. (Be careful not to cover the message at the bottom.)
9. Add star stickers on the stand-up.
10. Talk about how Martin Luther King, Jr. worked to make liberty and justice available to all people.

by Mary Tucker

TLC10280 Copyright © Teaching & Learning Company, Carthage, IL 62321-0010

Black Stars That Shine Brightly

Discuss some well-known African American people in show business, government, sports, science, etc. Then let students make this craft to honor those people and others like them.

Materials

star pattern
black construction paper
white chalk
gold or silver glitter
white, gold, or silver marker
scissors
glue
sharp pencil
yarn or string

Directions

1. Use white chalk to trace the star pattern from this page on black paper.
2. Cut out the black star.
3. Use a white, gold, or silver marker to neatly print the name of your favorite African American person and what that person does on the star.
4. Spread a thin layer of glue around the edge of the star.
5. Sprinkle glitter over the glue. Shake off excess glitter into a box or bag.
6. Use a sharp pencil to punch a small hole in the top of the star and add yarn or string to hang it up.
7. Hang your star over your desk.

by Mary Tucker

Patriotic Mobile

Have students make this mobile to celebrate Presidents' Day.

Materials

patterns of Lincoln, Washington, and U.S.A.
  (page 79)
white poster board
colored markers or crayons
string
scissors
hole punch

Directions

1. On half a sheet of white poster board, draw and color an American flag.
2. Trace the patterns of Lincoln, Washington, and the U.S.A. on the other half of the white poster board and cut them out.
3. Print on the back of the U.S.A. pattern why your're glad to be an American and your name.
4. Draw facial features and hair on the heads of Lincoln and Washington. Print their names on the backs of the heads.
5. Cut out four poster board squares, about 3" x 3". Print on one square the dates of Lincoln's presidency; on the other print the dates of Washington's presidency.
6. On the other two squares print a famous quote from each man or a fact about each one.
7. Punch holes in the top of all the pieces and hang them as shown with the information about the Presidents attached to the appropriate men.

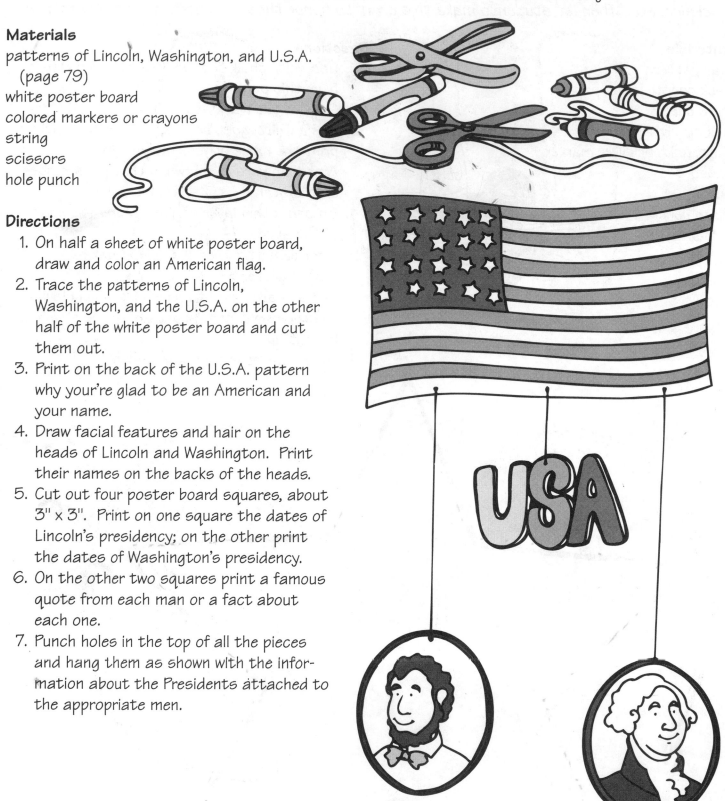

by Mary Tucker

Patriotic Mobile Patterns

Groundhog Day Shadow Rubbing

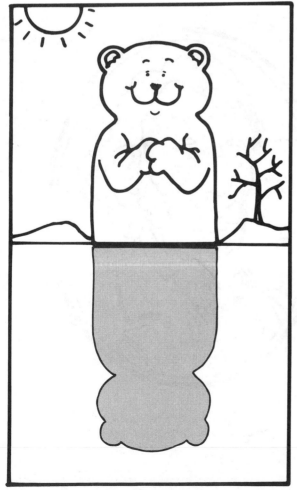

Reproduce the pattern. Color and cut out. Lay pattern under a sheet of thin paper. Gently rub with a pencil or crayon. Cut out the "shadow" around the outline created by the rubbing. Glue groundhog and shadow to a piece of paper, as shown. Add background or details as desired.

by Veronica Terrill

Valentine Activities
for Kids

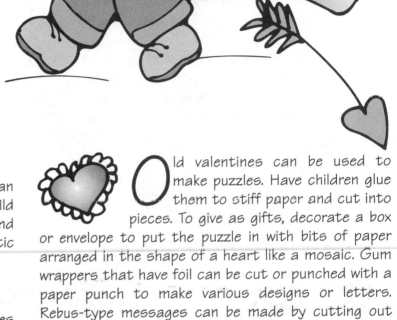

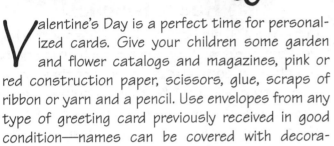

Valentine's Day is a perfect time for personal-ized cards. Give your children some garden and flower catalogs and magazines, pink or red construction paper, scissors, glue, scraps of ribbon or yarn and a pencil. Use envelopes from any type of greeting card previously received in good condition—names can be covered with decora-tions.

An empty box suitable for a wastebasket can result in an attractive gift. Have your child cover it with cut-out pictures, messages and drawings of their own. Covering it with clear plastic paper will make it useful for many years.

Make heart-shaped seed collages from kidney beans, colored pop-corn and other seeds that look like valentine colors. Cardboard or scraps of wood may be used as background and cov-ered or painted before seeds are glued on.

Have children think of gifts they can make from small seashells, pinecones and pebbles. Covering a can with these after applying red or pink paper will make a great pencil and pen holder for a desk. Lining it with adhesive plastic paper will add to its usefulness and appearance.

Old valentines can be used to make puzzles. Have children glue them to stiff paper and cut into pieces. To give as gifts, decorate a box or envelope to put the puzzle in with bits of paper arranged in the shape of a heart like a mosaic. Gum wrappers that have foil can be cut or punched with a paper punch to make various designs or letters. Rebus-type messages can be made by cutting out pictures or words from the valentines—for example, the picture of an eye would mean "I."

Gift booklets may be made from folded sheets held together with shoelaces, string or ribbon. They may hold whatever the child wants, such as pictures or poems. Encourage children to look in reference books and write down interesting facts about how Valentine's Day started, when cards were first sent, why it is called Valentine's Day, who Cupid is and why he has arrows. They can use short quota-tions or poems about love and friendship.

by Carol Smallwood

Fabulous Valentine Projects

Giant Heart "Cookies"

These "cookies" will look good enough to eat, but don't! Have the children cut a large heart shape from a Styrofoam™ tray. Let them paint the hearts red or pink. Allow the paint to dry; then have the children dribble glue here and there on their hearts. Sprinkle the glue with colored sugar and cake decorations or glitter and colored rice. Yum!?!

Heart Mobile

Cut several 3" squares of clear, self-adhesive paper. Peel the backing off of one for each child and have the children decorate the center of their squares with glitter, sequins, buttons, feathers or dried flowers. Cover their designs with a second piece of clear, self-adhesive paper and seal around the edges. Use a pattern and an ink pen to trace a heart shape around their designs. Have them cut out their hearts. Let them each make three. Punch a hole at the top of each heart, thread with a yarn length and knot. Punch three holes in a small, plastic margarine tub lid and tie the opposite ends of the yarn lengths through these holes. Tape a yarn loop to the center of the plastic lid for hanging.

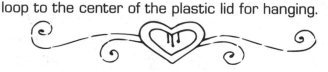

Fold-Over Heart

Have the children trace and cut a large white paper heart. Provide them with cotton swabs and red and white paints. Let them dab both colors of paint onto their hearts. Before the paint dries, help them fold their hearts in half and smooth them out with flat hands. Carefully re-open the hearts. Did anyone make a new color?

Valentine Breeze Catcher

Have the children wrap bath tissue tubes with red or pink tissue paper. Secure with tape. Let them each cut out two paper hearts and decorate with glitter. Let the glue dry, then staple the hearts to opposite sides of the tube. Tape or staple three red or pink crepe paper streamers to the bottom of the tube. Punch two holes on either side of the tube top and thread with red yarn for hanging.

by Marie Cecchini

Card Carriers

The children will love carrying their valentine card collections home in these cute little totes. Have them cut the top off of a paper lunch bag and help them fold down the new edge. The bags should be about half their original height. Provide the children with old valentine cards, glue and scissors. Let them cut designs, pictures and words from the old cards and glue them to the outside of their bags. Cut strips of thin cardboard and have the children decorate these with markers. Staple these handles to either side of the bag top.

"Candy" Hearts Basket

Twist the ends of a pipe cleaner through either side of a small, plastic produce basket to make a handle. Have the children trace and cut white Styrofoam™ hearts that are 2" to 3" across. Let them color both sides of the hearts with crayons, placing their hearts into their baskets as they are colored. Share some messages from real candy hearts, such as **yes, hug me** and **hi.** Help them use a narrow-tipped marker to write messages on their pretend candy hearts.

Party Place Mats

Have the children cut a large heart shape from white paper. Let them edge the heart with red or pink marker. Cut several vertical slits, about 1" apart, in their hearts. Provide them with red and pink paper strips to weave through the slits in their hearts.

Trim any strips that hang over the edge of the heart. Secure the ends of each strip with tape.

Heart Angels

For this project, each child will need one large heart, one small heart, two medium-sized hearts, a cardboard strip, a red pipe cleaner, markers, glue and tape. Place the large heart upside down (body), then glue the point of the small heart (head) to the point of the large heart. Glue the points of the medium-sized hearts (wings) to either side of the large heart. Decorate the cardboard strip with markers and staple it to the bottom of the body. Draw a face on each angel. Shape a circle at the top of the pipe cleaner and fold it forward to form a halo. Tape the bottom of the pipe cleaner to the back of the head.

Heart Flowers

Let the children each make two heart flowers by gluing a red or pink heart to the top of two pipe cleaners and two leaf shapes to either side of each pipe cleaner. Set these on waxed paper to dry. Help them make a vase by gluing an inverted Styrofoam™ cup onto a piece of cardboard for stability. Have an adult use a ballpoint pen to carefully poke two small holes in the cup. When the glue dries, help the children push their flower stems through the holes of their "vases."

Valentine's Day Quilt Card

Reproduce the pattern below onto heavy pink or pastel-colored paper. Color each "quilt" section a different color and/or pattern. Glue small buttons on, if desired. The heart can also be used as a pattern to cut "quilt blocks" out of wrapping paper.

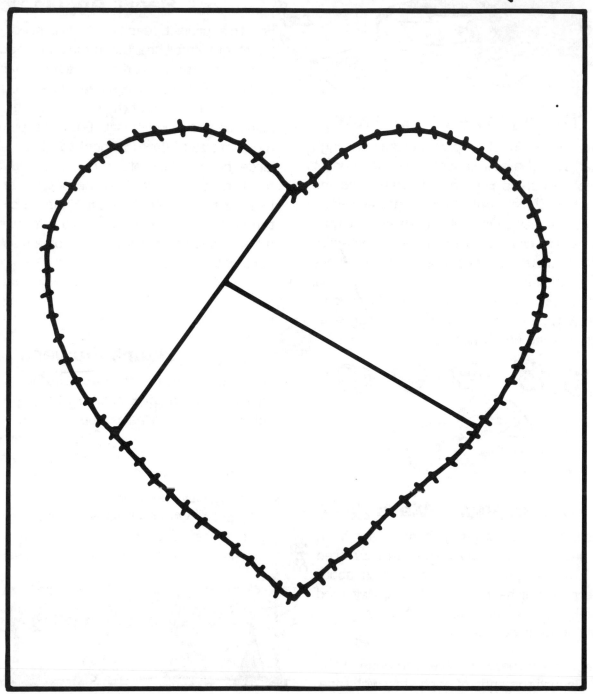

by Veronica Terrill

Peanut Projects

March is National Peanut Month.

Peanut Butter & Jelly Art

Cut out two bread shapes from white construction paper. Sponge-paint one using red paint for strawberry jelly or purple paint for grape jam. Paint the other slice light brown for the peanut butter. You can even mix a small amount of cornmeal into the paint for texture. Punch holes at the top and tie with a piece of yarn or secure the two shapes with a brad fastener.

Peanut Wreaths

Cut a circular wreath shape from heavy cardboard. Glue on an arrangement of peanuts (in shells) all around the wreath. There are many options for decorating: painting the shells, gluing on trims, glitter or a decorative bow. Tape a large paper clip to the back for a hanger.

Peanut Snack Tray

Glue an inverted foam cup between the bottom of a large plastic-coated plate and the top of a small plate or bowl. Decorate as desired. Use as a snack tray by placing peanuts on top and sliced fruit pieces on the bottom.

Peanut Puppet

Draw and cut a peanut shape out of brown paper. Next, cut rubber bands to make four equal pieces. Draw facial features on your peanut with crayons or markers. Wiggly eyes glued on would be quite humorous. On the back side, tape the rubber bands as arms and legs. Use another rubber band at the top as your manipulator. Pick up your peanut puppet by the top band and make him dance.

Peanut Printing

Use a whole peanut in its shell, a broken half shell and the peanut itself. Set out containers of tempera paint in various colors. Dip these products into the paint and make prints on white paper by pressing down on the peanut. Make random designs and use many colors for effect.

Peanut Photo Frame

Paste a favorite photo inside a jar lid. Glue this lid onto a larger circle of heavy cardboard. Decorate the larger circle with peanut shells. Paint and decorate as desired. Tape a large paper clip to the cardboard base as a hanger.

Edible Clay

Make a fun and edible clay from peanut butter.

2 cups peanut butter
1 cup honey
2 cups instant nonfat dry milk
wheat germ (optional—small amount for texture)

Mix these ingredients in a bowl with a spoon. With clean hands, let the children mold a share of this dough into all kinds of shapes: snakes, snowmen, creatures, etc. After the students are bored with this activity, they may eat their creations as a snack.

by Tania K. Cowling

A Good Day to Be Green!

Green Spin Art

Place a white paper plate in a cardboard box. Drop small drips of watery poster paints from a paintbrush onto the plate. Use blue and yellow paints to make green. Give the box a quick spin. With each spin, the design will change a bit.

Hearty Shamrock

Cut three hearts out of green construction paper. Form a shamrock by gluing the points of the hearts together on a separate piece of paper. Now, draw a stem or make one from construction paper. To decorate these shamrocks, make paper confetti (holes punched with a hole punch) out of all colors of construction paper. Glue these colorful dots randomly over the shamrock.

Shamrock Crown

Cut a band of heavy-duty paper or tagboard to fit around the child's head. Glue or staple the ends. Attach green pipe cleaners around the top edge of the crown. To the pipe cleaners, glue or staple construction paper shamrocks. Personalize these crowns by writing the child's name and *Happy St. Patrick's Day!*

Over the Rainbow

On a piece of black construction paper, draw six arches with chalk or a white crayon. Fill each arch by tearing small pieces of construction paper and gluing them down within the arch. Fill in the entire area of each arch as you follow this order of the rainbow: red, orange, yellow, green, blue, and purple.

by Tania Kourempis-Cowling

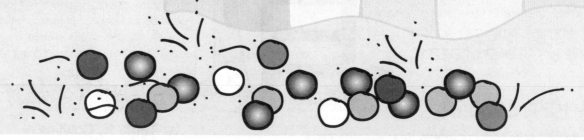

St. Patrick's Day Fun

Shamrock Flag

Let the children use a green marker to trace a large shamrock pattern on a 9" x 12" sheet of white paper. Have them sponge paint the shamrocks green. When dry, tape each flag to a cardboard paper towel tube.

Shamrock Shakers

Help the children use tape and green tissue paper to cover a bath tissue tube. Let them cut two circles from a brown paper bag. Secure one circle over an end of the tube with a rubber band. Have the children count out four or five dried peas and drop them into the open end of the tube. Secure the second circle over the open end with a rubber band. Provide shamrock stickers for the children to use to decorate their shakers.

Now put on some St. Patrick's Day music and have a parade with your flags and shakers.

Green Wall Hanging

Provide each child with glue and a strip of green paper about four inches wide. Poke two holes at the top of the paper and thread with green yarn for hanging. Supply a variety of green items, such as buttons, leaves, fabric scraps, pipe cleaners, beads, jug lids, yarn and sequins. Have them each create a green collage.

Dish Garden

Cut shamrock shapes from green sponges. Have the children moisten the sponges and set them in plastic lids. Provide them with grass seed to sprinkle on top. Keep the sponges moist and observe as the grass grows.

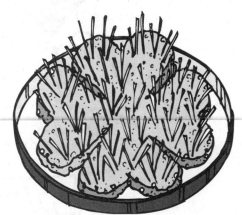

Name Necklaces

Provide small pre-cut shamrocks for the children. Have them count out as many shamrocks as there are letters in their names. Help them write each letter on a separate shamrock with white glue; then sprinkle green glitter over the glue. When the letters are dry, provide children with green yarn and large blunt needles. Show them how to string their shamrocks from side to side to spell their names. As they complete their necklaces, tie the yarn ends to secure.

Sprinkle Paint

Fill old saltshakers and spice bottles with blue and yellow tempera paint. Provide the children with these paint shakers, white paper and spray bottles filled with water. Have the children sprinkle both paint colors onto the white paper. Then spray the papers with water. Note any color mixing.

by Marie E. Cecchini

April Fools' Day
Silly Hats

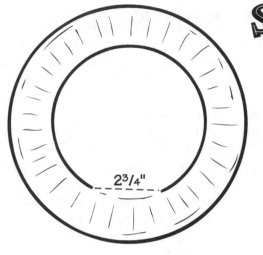

2³/₄"

Cut around the edge of a 9" paper plate, about 1³/₄" in from the edge, leaving 2³/₄" attached as shown. (Adjust the size of the circle as needed to fit child's head.) Attach ribbons or yarn to the sides of the plate as illustrated. Let the children decorate the plates, using pictures cut from magazines, glitter, pipe cleaners, bright markers and crayon, and even found objects. Encourage the children to be as "foolish" (silly) as possible as they create their hats.

by Veronica Terrill

Celebrate EARTH DAY

As we celebrate Earth Day, we become acutely aware of the many natural necessities we take so much for granted. As you discuss Earth Day with your class and take part in related activities, help them remember that taking care of our natural resources is a daily, lifelong process. Talk about ways you can celebrate Earth Day every day, right in the classroom, then follow through.

Brown Bag Posters

Have children cut brown grocery bags apart to form large rectangles. Provide markers or crayons and ask children to draw pictures of plants and/or animals on one rectangle, creating a poster. Let them frame the drawings by using magazine pictures of plants and animals, or by tracing and cutting plant and animal shapes from scrap paper. Display the posters within the classroom and throughout the school.

Earth Day Flags

Cut smaller rectangles from brown grocery bags for this activity. After you've discussed Earth Day and some of the ways people can work together to make Earth cleaner, have children create pictures on the rectangles depicting ways they feel they can help. Encourage them to develop appropriate slogans for their flags. Write the slogans on their flags. Tape or staple each flag to a paper towel tube. Then lead them an Earth Day parade, waving the flags and playing some of nature's instruments, such as sticks or rocks for banging and scraping, and gourds for shaking.

by Marie E. Cecchini

Save That Junk

When Earth Day arrives in April, it's time to teach concepts on the preservation of our planet. Children need to learn how important it is to conserve natural resources, reduce the amount of garbage and to recycle. In our classrooms, we can encourage students to save and collect supplies rather than buying new products. The idea is to "save that junk" and turn throwaways into creative and fun art media.

What to Collect

boxes—all sizes
egg and milk cartons
berry boxes—paper and plastic
twine and string
cardboard tubes
salt and oatmeal boxes
straws
old magazines and catalogs
cotton
Styrofoam™ pieces and trays
wire and hangers
fabric and trims
glass jars
plastic containers and bottles
clothespins
lumber scraps
aluminum foil and cans
nature items
nylon stockings
nuts and bolts
clock parts
cancelled stamps

The list is endless!

Nifty Newspaper Art

Glue a piece of newspaper (a classified page looks great) onto an 8" x 10" piece of cardboard. Plan a picture, a garden of flowers, a clown with balloons or maybe a train with a trail of boxcars, just to name a few. Cut out pieces from colorful felt, fabric, trims, wallpaper and magazine pages. Glue these onto the cardboard. You have now created a design that stands out from its newsprint background.

by Tania Kourempis-Cowling

Puppets

There are endless possibilities to make puppets from the recycle bin. Bases could be old socks, tin cans, margarine tubs, dish detergent bottles, oatmeal/salt boxes and the standard lunch bag.

Boxy Puzzles

Take the front panel from a favorite cereal or cookie box. Cut this into zigzag puzzle pieces. The amount of pieces and difficulty vary according to the age of the students. Code the back of each piece with a number or symbol and store these in a locking plastic bag.

Can Shakers

Make rhythm shakers or noisemakers with empty aluminum soda cans. Put dried beans or small pebbles inside; tape the opening shut. Cover the entire can with aluminum foil. Press the foil securely around the can. Decorate with colorful stickers and stars.

Stencil Fun

Plastic lids from margarine tubs and coffee cans make great stencils. Cut out geometric shapes, animals, stars or any favorite design. The kids can use these stencils to trace shapes and color pictures.

Earth-Friendly Art

Objective: Create a visual reminder to be Earth friendly. Show how "junk" can be reused to make something new.

Make a "Junk-a-Saurus"

Materials: Have children bring in empty cans, toilet paper/paper towel rolls, shoe/tissue boxes, empty soda pop/milk/detergent plastic bottles, empty thread spools, old yarn, buttons, any other "junk" found around the house.

Talk about dinosaurs, especially their shapes. Discuss how models could be made using the junk. Let each child design and "build" her own Junk-a-saurus, fastening it together with paste, tape or brackets. When finished, she should give it a name and make up a story. Put all finished creatures together in a display.

I-Love-Nature Mobile

Materials: magazines from which to cut pictures and/or drawing paper on which to draw pictures of sun, rain, grass, tree, flower, bird, ocean, lake, fish, wild animal, soil; crayons/markers; paper straws; thread or thin string; scissors; glue; cardboard

In class, discuss the gifts nature gives us. List them on the board. The list should include those mentioned above but children may have other suggestions, too. Let each student make his own mobile, including as many things from the list as he wishes. Hang mobiles in the classroom before taking them home.

Wear-a-Message T-Shirts

Materials: old, solid-color T-shirts; permanent color markers/crayons; big pieces of cardboard

Together in class make a list of Earth-friendly sayings. Have each student choose a saying and (on scrap paper) design a simple picture using words and/or designs. Stretch T-shirt over cardboard and, using markers or crayons (or a combination), draw the same picture on the front of the T-Shirt. Some may want to do the back, too. If marker is used, let it dry on the cardboard. If crayon is used, put a piece of brown craft paper on top and apply hot iron to set color. Have a Wear-Your-T-shirt Day, perhaps having a parade through other classes. The recycled T-shirt can be washed and worn again and again!

by Elaine Hansen Cleary

Egg Crafts

Egg Craft
Turn eggshells into egg art with this outdoor craft project.

Materials
- one sheet of cardboard or heavy tagboard per student
- white glue and thin paintbrushes
- butcher's string
- scissors
- eggshells
- food coloring or egg dye
- cups
- spoons
- waxed paper
- rolling pins

Procedure
1. Draw an egg shape on your cardboard or tagboard.
2. Cut a length of string that will go around the circumference of your egg.
3. Paint or squeeze a trail of glue over the circumference of your egg shape and lay the string on top to form an outline of the egg.
4. Mix your egg dyes or food colors in cups. Dip the eggshells in the various colors.
5. When the eggshells have dried, place one color at a time between two sheets of waxed paper.
6. Roll over the waxed paper with a rolling pin until the shells are crushed.
7. Place the colored shells in cups.

8. Paint the inside of your egg shape with a thick layer of glue. Gluing can be done one section at a time, or all at once, depending upon the design you hope to achieve.
9. Sprinkle the colored eggshells in a pattern or kaleidoscope of color onto the glued surface. When one area is dry, another area can be glued and sprinkled with eggshells.
10. Let the finished egg dry indoors until completely hardened and then shake the excess shells from your masterpiece.
11. Make a mixture of half glue and half water to paint lightly over the the eggshells.

by Robynne Eagan

Lunch Bag Easter Basket

Here's an Easter basket made from a paper lunch bag that is both easy and inexpensive to make.

Materials: paper lunch bag (brown or white), scissors, glue, crayons or markers, string (optional), precut patterns the size of the lunch bag

Directions:
Close the lunch bag, having folds at the bottom (A) and top (B). Place pattern on bag. Just above fold (B) start tracing solid lines. Cut on solid lines. (You will be cutting double.) One side will be the front of the bunny, the other side the back. Color a face and bow tie, and glue string whiskers on the front side. Glue a cotton ball tail on the back side. Glue or tape tips of ears together to form the handle.

Basket can be filled with "grass" and lightweight candies or crackers.

(D)

Glue front and back tips of each ear to form handle.

Cut double on *solid black lines* only.

Do not cut folds (dotted lines).

(C)
(B) Fold of bottom of bag

Side

Side

(A) Fold up bottom of bag

by Elaine Hansen Cleary

Easter "Egg"citement

Materials

- egg shape template
- heavy bond art paper
- masking tape
- crayons
- variety of paints (see recipes on this page)
- brightly colored construction paper
- white glue and glue brushes
- scissors
- paint shirts for children

Let's Make It

1. Prepare a variety of textured paints.
2. Prepare a large flat work surface that allows children room for carefree expression.
3. Provide templates or samples of egg shapes and sizes.

What to Do

1. Have children draw or trace egg shapes on their papers.
2. Children will decorate the eggs with the various paints and textures.
3. When the paint dries, children can cut out their egg shapes and paste them to brightly colored pieces of construction paper with the words _____'s Eggs printed across the top.

Bailey's Eggs

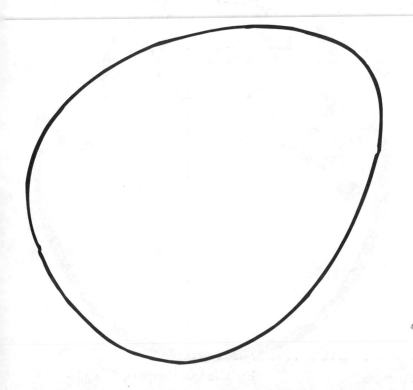

Glitter Squeeze Paint

Materials

- 1 cup (250 ml) flour
- 1 cup (250 ml) salt
- 1 cup (250 ml) water
- food coloring
- spoon
- bowls
- squeeze-top bottles
- funnel

Preparation

1. Mix flour, salt and water together in bowl until well mixed.
2. Divide the mixture into small bowls and add food coloring to each batch until you achieve the desired colors.
3. Use the funnel to help you pour the paint into squeeze bottles.
4. Children will squeeze this paint onto the paper.
5. Let dry thoroughly.

by Robynne Eagan

An Easter Egg Surprise

Materials

- egg patterns
- heavy paper
- scissors
- crayons or colored markers
- brass brad fastener
- glue and glitter (optional)

Directions

1. Copy the egg patterns on heavy paper for each child.

2. Have children color the chick and the two egg pieces. Encourage them to be creative in how they color the egg. Let them spread glue over the egg and add glitter if they want.

3. Help children cut out the egg pieces.

4. Poke a brad fastener through the black dot on each egg piece to fasten them together.

5. Show children how they can lift up the top half of the egg to reveal the surprise (the chick).

by Mary Tucker

Easter Bonnet

Easter bonnet
With everything on it.

Bonnets with cherries,
Grapes, and blueberries.

Bonnets with lace
And a funny face.

Wide-rimmed bonnets
With flowers,
You seem to make
For hours.

Many bonnets are white.
Others are blue
And yellow too.

Happy, happy Easter to you.

Paper Plate Easter Bonnet

Materials

paper plate	stapler
scissors	crayons
ribbon	lace
masking tape	colored tissue paper

Directions

1. Color paper plate or draw pictures on one side.

2. Cut five 3" squares of tissue paper per flower.

3. Place the squares together and accordion fold several times.

4. Pinch-fold squares together in the middle, and staple to colored side of paper plate.

5. Arrange stapled squares into flowers by gently separating each individual layer.

6. Cut several small pieces of masking tape. Use the tape to cover sharp edges of staples on bonnet; then color tape.

7. Cut two 12" pieces of lace or ribbon, and staple one piece to each side of bonnet.

8. Place Easter bonnet on head and tie under chin.

You can make as many paper plate Easter bonnets as you have paper plates and supplies! Use an assortment of tissue paper, ribbon, lace, and other art supplies to make each bonnet different.

by E.E. Stewart

Earth-Friendly
Easter Baskets

Half-Pint Milk or Juice Cartons

These make great individual baskets. Just coat half-pint milk or juice cartons with glue; then attach decorations from your scrap box: bits of felt, colored paper scraps, wallpaper scraps, yarn bows, stickers, old buttons, small plastic flowers, small pictures cut from old greeting cards . . . almost anything children like. Attach a cardboard or ribbon handle using glue or staples. Bits of torn or shredded scrap paper, reused tissue, or wrapping paper can be used as grass.

Margarine or Whipped Topping Containers

These make neat baskets. Decorate the containers the same way as the cartons above, or coat with glue and wrap yarn around and around from top to bottom. For a nutritious snack, line the "baskets" with lettuce leaves and fill with fresh fruit pieces or raw veggies!

cut out

Lunch Bag Baskets

Reuse lunch bags that have been carefully saved—not wrinkled or torn (or use new bags). Fold bag in at the sides and up from the bottom following the crease that is already there. Trace the pattern on the left on the bag and cut (you'll be cutting double). Draw a bunny face on one side. Glue a small pink pom-pom or cut out a small pink circle for the nose. Glue yarn or thread whiskers to the nose. Make two ears and glue in place. Put a cotton tail on the back.

by Elaine Hansen Cleary

Hint: Ask parents to send in bits and pieces to use for decorations. Best of all, these baskets can all be recycled when no longer in use!

Stand-Up Bunny

Lay pattern on a folded 5" x 8" sheet of pastel colored construction paper and cut out on solid lines. Use a paper punch to punch eye holes. Glue rabbit to a covered paper roll. Decorate with plastic grass, pipe cleaner "whiskers," and so on as desired. (Label with child's name before assembling, to use a place marker.)

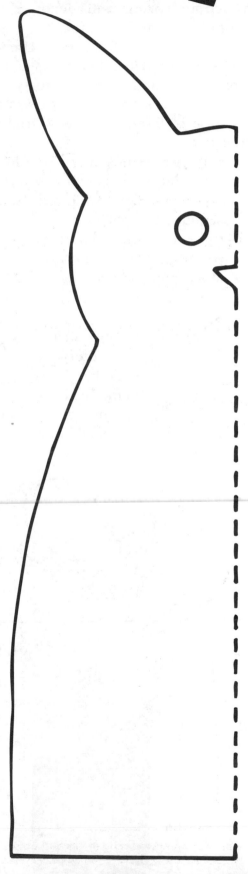

"Egg"citing Ideas

Let Egg Trees Bloom

Welcome spring and decorate your room at the same time . . . with trees full of eggs. Use small limbs anchored in coffee cans filled with small rocks and water. (If forsythia is available, that's even better!) Use a combination of these methods to trim your tree:

- Cut egg shapes from Styrofoam™ trays and decorate with bits from the scrap box (yarn, foil, felt, buttons, sequins, beads, ribbons).
- Cut egg shapes from patterned wallpaper glued to cardboard.
- Make papier-mâché eggs and paint them in pastel colors (for older children).
- Form foil into egg shapes (and be sure to recycle it afterward).
- Cut out construction paper eggs and write on them: reading, spelling, social studies, or science words; numbers facts; kind words, Easter wishes, or short poems; rhyming words, homonyms, or homographs.

by Elaine Hansen Cleary

Hatching Chick

Glue one half of an eggshell to a small square of poster board. In the center of the shell, glue a large yellow pom-pom. On top of that, glue a smaller yellow pom-pom. Add two wiggly eyes and an orange paper beak, and you have a cute baby chick ready for Easter.

Eggshell Plant Pots

Collect and crush at least 12 empty eggshells for each student. Spread glue on the sides of a metal can. Roll the can in the eggshells and allow it to dry completely. Paint the can with acrylic paints, fill it with dirt and add a pretty plant.

Mr. Egg

This project requires blown eggshells. This isn't hard for children to do, as long as you remind them not to pretend they are a hurricane.

Have each student carefully poke a tiny hole in the small end of an egg. Have them poke a larger hole in the bigger end. Over a sink (or bowl, if you wish to keep the egg's insides), have the child *gently* blow on the small end until the egg's yolk and white slide out the larger hole. Wash the empty eggshell carefully.

Mr. Egg is made by first decorating a toilet tissue tube with construction paper clothes. You can add buttons, rickrack or other materials.

Next paste facial features on the eggshell or draw them on with markers. Add some yarn for hair. Then attach the eggshell to the cardboard tube. These make cute puppets. You might consider using them in a springtime skit.

by Donna Stringfellow

100

Decorated Eggs

Students can decorate eggs using white glue and many common household products.

1. Cut out several egg shapes from cardboard using the pattern on the right. Students will use this to trace.

2. After students trace the egg shape on white paper, they can decorate it by drawing lines, circles, faces, zigzags or other designs.

3. Apply white glue (the kind in a squeeze bottle works best) to one part of the design. Sprinkle one of the suggested items on the glue. Let that dry and shake off the excess. Apply glue to another section of the design and sprinkle another item on that section. Continue until the eggs are completely decorated.

4. Students can cut out the finished eggs after they dry and hang them from a tree or use them as classroom decorations.

Note: This project can be rather messy. You might want to spread newspaper over a large table and let students work together in one area rather than at individual desks.

Items to use for decorating eggs:

seashells

uncooked rice

colored sand or gravel

Cheerios™, Rice Krispies™ or other types of dry cereal

sunflower seeds or other small seeds

uncooked macaroni or other noodles

various colored dried beans

popped popcorn

colored sugar

peanuts

by Cindy Barden

101

Bunny Land

Invite your children to hop on over to "Bunny Land" for some fun-filled Easter activities.

Bunny Bracelet

Cut several 1" circular strips from a cardboard tube. Slice each strip so it will open. Provide the children with white paper, scissors, markers and a small bunny pattern. Have them trace, color and cut out their bunnies. Staple each bunny to a cardboard strip. Open the strip and slide it onto the child's wrist. (scissor skills)

Box Garden

Make use of shoe box lids, green paper and garden catalogs to "plant" a garden fit for a rabbit. Cut the green paper into strips. Have the children use scissors to fringe the strips for grass. Glue this grass around the edges of the lid, forming a framed, rectangular garden area. Let the children cut fruit and vegetable pictures from the garden catalogs to plant in their gardens with glue. (scissor skills)

Baby Bunny Baskets

Baskets: Punch a hole in both sides of a one-pound margarine tub. Fasten the ends of a pipe cleaner through the holes to make a handle. Let the children decorate the containers with Easter stickers. Place Easter grass in each basket.

Baby Bunny: Glue two cotton balls together, one on top of the other, to form a bunny head and body. Glue two small pink ears to the back of the head. Add two black hole-punch eyes, a pink triangle nose, yarn-snip whiskers and a yarn snip mouth. Place the baby bunny in its basket to dry.

(small motor skills, following directions)

by Marie E. Cecchini

Bunny in a Hole

Cut oatmeal or salt boxes in half. Cover the cylinder with green paper, poke a hole in the bottom and fill with Easter grass. Have each child cut out a small bunny from pink or white paper and color it. Tape the bunny to the top of a drinking straw or craft stick. Slide the opposite end of the straw or stick through the hole under the grass. The children can then hold the box in one hand and move the straw or stick with the other hand to make the bunny hop into and up from the grass.

Bunny Beenies

Provide the children with disposable plastic bowls to decorate with Easter stickers. Poke a hole in both sides of the bowl, thread with elastic cord and tie to fit under each child's chin. Have the children color and cut out their own bunnies. Tape each bunny to the top of a pipe cleaner. Poke the opposite end of the pipe cleaner through the hat and tape it to the inside. The bunnies will wiggle and hop when the children wear their beenies.

Bunny Cups

Make cute Bunny Cups for storing tiny treasures or colorful jelly beans. Supply the children with Styrofoam™ cups, pink paper, pink pom-poms, black pipe cleaners, scissors, glue and markers. Have them draw eyes on the cup and cut out two pink ears to glue at the top. Let them glue on a pom-pom nose and cut out a pink mouth to glue at the bottom. When the glue is dry, poke both ends of a pipe cleaner from the inside of the cup to the outside on either side of the nose for whiskers. Bend to shape. Add a second pipe cleaner in the same manner.

Springy Fun

Faces in Our Garden

Paper cupcake/muffin liners create flowers with a three-dimensional effect. Cut petals, stems and leaves from bright colored construction paper. Paste liners in center of flowers, with school pictures of students in the center.

Circle Learning

Learn about life within a circle by placing a Hula-Hoop™ (or a rope circle with a three-foot diameter) in a grassy area. Using magnifying glasses, search for insects. Identify by looking up different species in a children's reference book.

by Carolyn Ross Tomlin

Flower Wind Sock

For each child, cut a 1" x 12" strip of thin cardboard (such as a cereal box). Have children glue green crepe paper over one side of the cardboard strip. Provide children with scrap paper, markers, scissors, and glue, and let them design flowers to glue onto the crepe paper. You may also choose to have them glue on some flowers from the artificial flower collection. Allow the glue to dry, then have children glue three or four 12" crepe paper streamers to the back of the cardboard, spacing them evenly. Staple the cardboard strips into circular shapes, then have children design additional paper flowers (or use artificial flowers), gluing one to the bottom of each streamer. Use a hole punch to make three holes in the cardboard circle. Tie a length of yarn through each hole; then gather the opposite ends of the yarn and tie them together to create a hanger for the wind sock.

by Marie Cecchini

104

Celebrating Mardi Gras

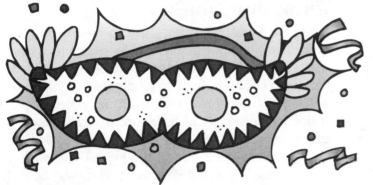

Mardi Gras Masks

Students can make their own masquerade masks from poster board. Cut out a mask shape. Collect decorating trims in the festive colors of purple, green and yellow (gold). Glue on sequins, feathers, glitter, lace and so on. Attach a piece of elastic to the back of the mask with a stapler so it will fit the child's head.

Toy Floats

Gather several boxes of different sizes (jewelry boxes are perfect for this project). Cover these with tissue or construction paper in Mardi Gras colors. Glue the boxes together to make a float replica. Add decorative trims, make paper flags, use stickers, attach plastic people or animals—all to make an authentic-looking parade float. Place the children's floats along a shelf to make a street parade display.

King Puppets

You will need:

- 1 shoulder pad (removed from an old sweater or blouse; colored fabric ones are best)
- round Styrofoam™ ball or Ping-Pong™ ball
- tacky glue or low temperature glue gun
- toothpick
- paint and markers
- lace, rickrack, trims, etc.
- chenille strips

Fold the shoulder pad ends to meet in the center. Glue these together to look like a robe. You can also glue on trims, buttons and so on to make the character. Paint facial features onto the round ball. Poke a toothpick into the ball and then insert this head into the top edge of the shoulder pad puppet. Glue this into place. Arms can be made by wrapping chenille strips (pipe cleaners) around the head portion and shaping these into arms. The child can then place their finger into the bottom edge of the shoulder pad to manipulate their puppet's actions.

by Tania K. Cowling

Junk Jug Shaker

Make a parade even more festive by creating rattling sounds to go with the music. A homemade instrument that could add these sounds would be a "junk jug shaker." Each child will need an empty milk or juice jug with a handle. Then have fun collecting objects to place inside for noises. Items like wooden beads, jingle bells, dried beans, pennies, pebbles and so on could be used. Apply glue to the inside of the jug lid before screwing it into place. Have the children hold the jug by its handle and shake it up and down as they march around the room.

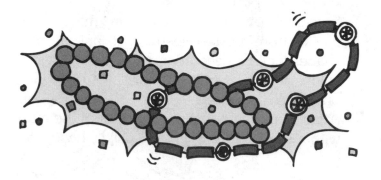

Bead Necklaces

There are two types of homemade necklaces that can easily be made in the classroom. You can make a clay mixture and roll beads, or string colorful pasta. Here is one recipe for salt dough (there are many others in art books). Mix 1 cup salt, $1/2$ cup cornstarch and $3/4$ cup water in a pan. Stir these ingredients over low heat. After the mixture has thickened, in about three minutes or so, place it onto waxed paper. Let the dough cool slightly and then proceed to knead it until smooth. Roll the dough into small balls and push a plastic straw through the center to make a threading hole. Allow the beads to air dry thoroughly.

Optional: Purchase multicolored pasta or tint regular pasta by using food coloring. Dip the pasta into a bowl containing water, food coloring and a teaspoon of rubbing alcohol. Leave the pasta in this mixture only long enough for the pasta to tint, and then quickly remove it to air dry on waxed paper. Thread the beads or pasta onto a length of yarn. Tie the ends together after measuring around the child's head for size.

106

A Basket for May Day

Each child will enjoy making this simple basket and hanging it on a friend's door for May Day. You'll need to help staple the paper plates together.

Materials

- 2 paper saucers
- crayons
- stapler and staples
- glue
- glitter
- hole punch
- ribbon or yarn
- Easter basket grass
- small treats to put in the basket (gum, flowers, stickers, candy and so on)

Directions

1. Give each child two paper saucers. Help them cut one in half.

2. Have them color the saucer and half saucer, adding glue and glitter to make them sparkle.

3. Staple the half saucer to the whole saucer (front to front) leaving the top open to make a pocket.

4. Punch two holes in the top of the whole paper plate and tie ribbon or yarn in them for a hanger.

5. Let each child fill the basket with Easter grass and small treats.

by Mary Tucker

May Day Flowers

May Day Bouquet

Materials

fresh spring flowers (violets, daffodils, lilacs, daisies)	paper doily (purchased or hand-made)
aluminum foil	paper tissue or cotton wool
ribbon	rubber bands

Directions

The first day of May is the day to give flowers to a special friend. It is easy to make a small bouquet, or nosegay, of fresh flowers. First pick a few fresh flowers like those mentioned above. Leave the stems long and include some leaves.

Arrange the flowers into a small pleasing bouquet. Put a rubber band around the stems, close to the flowers, to hold the bouquet in place. Cut the stems so they are even at the bottom of your bouquet. Now wrap wet paper tissue or cotton wool around the cut stems to keep the flowers fresh. Cover the wet tissue with aluminum foil.

Push the aluminum foil-covered stems through the center of a paper doily. (Make a doily by cutting a lacy pattern in a circle or paper.) Finally, tie a ribbon around the bouquet just below the doily and your May Day nosegay is ready to give.

May Day Basket

Materials

ice-cream cones	ribbon or yarn
small paper doily	fabric scraps
spray starch	pipe cleaners

Directions

Cut several simple flower shapes from fabric scraps. Spray with spray starch to add stiffness to the petals. Make a tiny hole in the center of each flower and push a pipe cleaner through the hole for a stem.

Carefully make two holes in the upper part of an ice-cream cone. Run ribbon or yarn through these holes for a hanger. Push the pipe cleaner stems through the center of a paper doily. Arrange flowers and doily into the ice-cream cone. On May Day hang the bouquet on the doorknob of someone you love.

by D.A. Woodliff

A Mexican Fiesta

Activities to Bring Mexican Customs to Your Classroom

Mexican Table Toppers

by Tania Kourempis-Cowling

Tie-Dyed Flowers

You will need about three or four paper coffee filters per flower. Using several containers, place several drops of food coloring into a tablespoon of water. Fold the filter into quarters. Dip one end into the mixture, letting it absorb color. Continue dipping the other filters in different colors. Lay these filters flat to dry. Later, place all filters on top of one another. Gather them together at the bottom and wrap a pipe cleaner tightly around the end for the stem. Place these around the room in vases or attach to walls.

Place Mats
(Mantelitos)

Make a place mat out of construction paper to set a Mexican table for either snack or lunch. Use the Mexican flag colors of red, white and green. Fold an 8½" x 11" piece of construction paper lengthwise. Cut slits up from the fold. Stop cutting about ½" from the edge of the paper. Make the slits an inch or so apart. Open. Now, weave construction paper strips over and under the slits of the place mat. Tape all the ends down to secure. Decorate the border any way you choose.

Yarn Napkin Rings

Using yarn to make colorful pictures, a famous art form in Mexico. Instead of pictures, this project will correlate with the above place mat to set a Mexican table. The napkin ring consists of a piece of toilet tube about 3" long. Spread glue on the outside of the tube, and wrap colorful yarn around the cylinder. Pass a napkin through the holder when it's dry.

Mexican Party Favors

Bag Pinata

A pinata is a decorated container usually filled with candy and small toys. The children play a traditional game, blindfolded, to break the pinata and let out all the "goodies." The first pinatas were made of clay but now papier-mâché ones have been substituted. A simple pinata for the classroom can be made from a paper grocery bag. Have the children decorate the bag as they wish with art materials. Open the bag and fold down the top a few times. Punch a hole on opposite sides of the top of the bag and thread ribbon or yarn through for a hanger. It's fun to add crepe paper streamers or ribbons to the bottom edge. These can be taped, glued or stapled on. Fill the bag with "goodies." Hang it from the ceiling or a doorway and proceed to play the pinata game with your students.

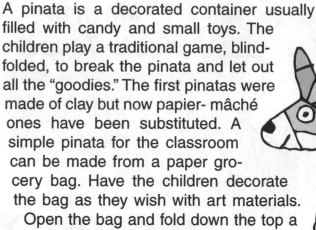

Mosaic

A mosaic is defined as a surface decoration made by inlaying small pieces of variously colored materials to form pictures or patterns. Try to obtain pictures of Mexican mosaics from books in the library or a local museum. Famous Mexican artists specializing in mosaic are Alfaro Sequeiros, Diego Rivera and Rufino Tamayo.

Make a classroom or individual mosaic using lasagna pasta. Paint the lasagna strips with tempera paint. Paint different strips various colors. When dry, break the strips into pieces. On a square of cardboard, draw a simple picture or design. Glue the pieces onto the square fitting them close together.

110

STICK PUPPET MINI PIÑATA

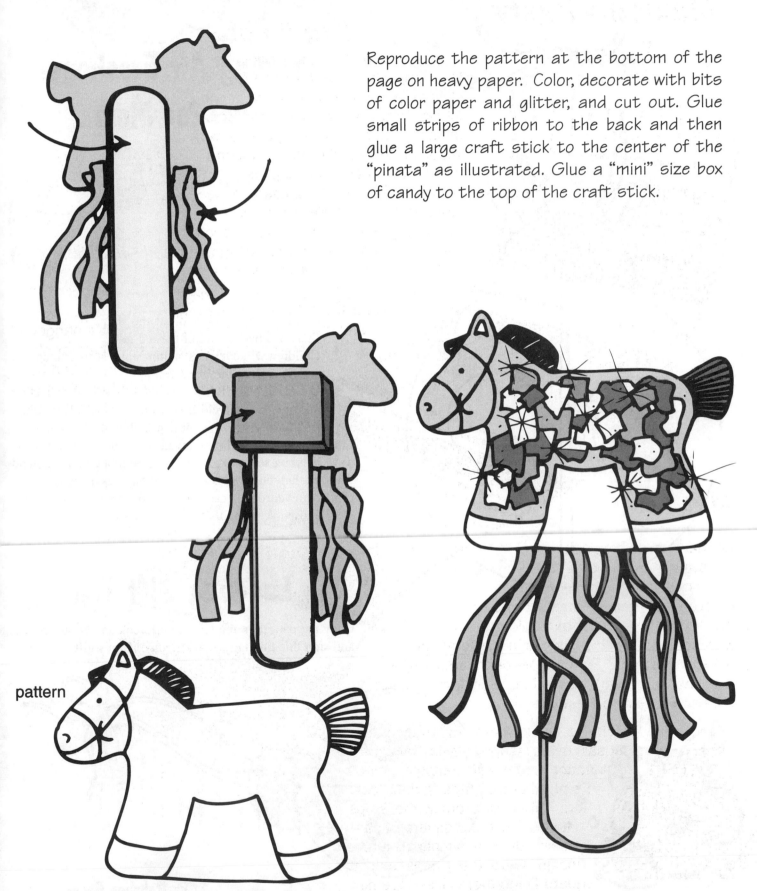

Reproduce the pattern at the bottom of the page on heavy paper. Color, decorate with bits of color paper and glitter, and cut out. Glue small strips of ribbon to the back and then glue a large craft stick to the center of the "pinata" as illustrated. Glue a "mini" size box of candy to the top of the craft stick.

pattern

BY VERONICA TERRILL

Ladybug Air Freshener Just for Mom

Materials

8" x 8" (20 x 20 cm) square of red felt
4" x 4" (10 x 10 cm) square of black felt
glue gun and glue sticks
black marker
hole punch
length of wool or string
small vials of essential oils (lavender, cinnamon, rose, or orange)
small eyedropper

Let's Make It

1. Children will draw and cut the shape of a ladybug (ladybird beetle) out of the red felt.
2. Children will cut spots, a thin center stripe, antennae, and eyes from the black felt.
3. Details in black felt will be glued to the red felt using the glue gun. If children find this too challenging, smaller parts may be drawn with a black marker.
4. A hole should be punched on a chosen spot on the ladybug so that the string can be looped through and the ladybug will balance and hang as desired.
5. An eyedropper can be used to drop tiny drops of a chosen scent on this charming air freshener.

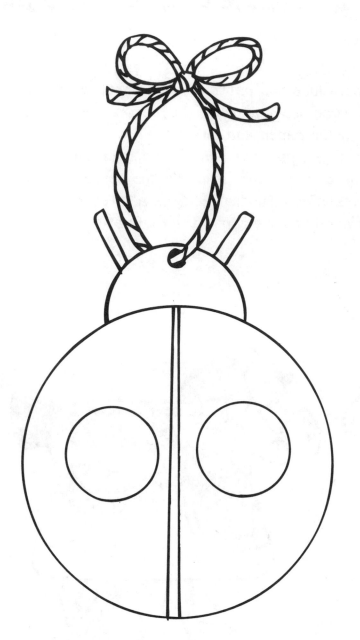

Ladybug Gift Tag

Copy the pattern at the left so children can cut out, color, and sign this tiny tag to accompany Mom's gift.

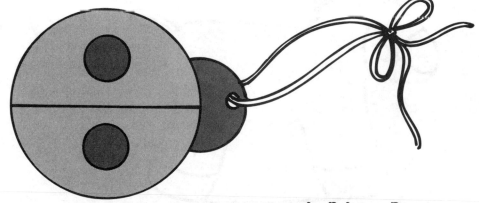

by Robynne Eagan

Pop-Out Mother's Day Card (Front)

fold →

1. Use reproducible sheets for the front and inside of cards.
2. Use construction paper or lightweight cardboard for the cards. Color the pictures.
3. Use construction paper or lightweight cardboard for "pop-outs."
4. Paste "pop-outs" on cards on the places marked with Xs.

by Sister M. Yvonne Moran

Pop-Out Mother's Day Card (Inside)

fold →

Dear Mom,

I give you these flowers.
I want them all to say—

Happy Mother's Day!

114

Super Soap Dispenser

Collect clean, empty liquid soap and hand lotion dispensers. Provide students with wallpaper scraps, glue, scissors, and bits of sewing trim. Allow students to decorate their containers as they choose. When dry, fill the dispenser or send it home to fill. These creative soap dispensers make wonderful additions to any home or office.

Gifts of Love for *Mother's Day*

Personal Calendars

Let your children design keepsake calendars for holiday gift giving. Provide each child with a 12" x 18" sheet of construction paper, and a 1½" x 12" strip of poster board. Help children place the poster board strip over one 12" side of the paper, hold in place, and use a hole punch to pierce two holes through both papers. Have children glue this strip across the 12" side, matching holes. Next, use a paintbrush and tempera to color both palms of each child. Help children press both hands to either side of the paper, just above the center. Allow the paint to dry, then provide children with markers to make a self-portrait in the section between their hands. Copy 12 blank calendar pages for each child. Help them to fill in the name and numerals for each month. Staple these pages to the bottom half of the 12" x 18" paper.

Patchwork Plant Packs

Here's an easy mini garden delight suitable for many occasions. First, have children glue fabric scraps around the outside of a plastic planter, giving it the look of a patchwork quilt. Next, let children spoon potting soil into sandwich bags, securing the tops with twist ties. When the glue is dry, have each student place a bag of soil into a pot, tuck in a pack of seeds, and then use paper, markers, scissors, tape, and a craft stick to design a plant label. Instruct children to place the signs in the pots, then help them wrap the entire pot with plastic wrap. Cinch the plastic wrap at the top with ribbon, then add a gift card.

by Marie E. Cecchini

Keepsake Glitter Box

Try this simple craft and make shining treasure or trinket boxes for friends or family members. Have children contribute small gift boxes with lids. Show them how to use a small paintbrush to spread glue over the entire box top. Help them sprinkle glitter over the glue. Allow to dry. In a well-ventilated place, spray clear acrylic sealer on the box tops to seal the glitter.

Button Bookmarks

Try these quick, easy, yet very classy, bookmark gifts. Provide each child with a 12" length of ribbon (at least 1 1/2" wide), glue, and an assortment of buttons. Have children fold over and glue the top and bottom edges of the ribbon to prevent fraying, then have them glue one or two buttons at the top and the bottom. Allow the glue to dry, then let the children try out the bookmarks in a library book before wrapping.

Variation: You might want to have older students use needles and thread to stitch the ends down, and sew the buttons on.

Potpourri Pouches

Have the children stitch up their own pouches and mix up their own potpourri for a delightfully fragrant gift. Have each child contribute one citrus fruit or apple and a small amount of a fragrant spice, such as cinnamon or cloves. Peel the fruits and set the skins in a warm, dry place for several days to dry. Use the fruit to make a fruit salad snack. To make the pouches, provide each child with a 4" x 10" piece of burlap, a tapestry needle, and yarn. Help children fold the burlap in half to measure 4" x 5", and have them sew a running stitch up each side about 1/2" in from the edge. Knot the yarn ends to secure. Show them how to pull off individual strands of burlap to fringe the sides. To make the potpourri, break the dried fruit rinds into small pieces and place them in a bowl. Sprinkle the rinds with the spices and mix gently. Fill each pouch about half full with the potpourri. Cinch the top and secure with yarn.

Pull off individual strands of burlap to fringe the top.

Mother's Day Painted Pots

Materials

terra-cotta planting pots (any size)
acrylic paints
paintbrushes or sponges
clear acrylic sealer
card
hole punch
ribbon

Let's Make It

1. If using old pots, clean and dry them thoroughly before painting.
2. Have children paint the pots in their own creative way. Demonstrate various methods of painting. Paintbrushes can be used to paint dots, stripes, or other designs. Toothbrushes can be rubbed to create splatter designs. Sponge shapes might be dipped in paint to create prints. Small fingers and hands can be dipped in paint and pressed on the pot to make personal prints.
3. When the paint has dried, take the pots to an outdoor area, away from children, and spray with acrylic sealer. Allow to dry thoroughly.
4. Have children fill pots with flower seeds or flowering plants.
5. Each child can decorate a card and then punch a hole in it. Ribbon can be threaded through the hole and tied around the pot. (Print this message on the card.)

My mom is very special
in so many ways.
My love for her is like this plant—
it grows every day.

Love, _____

My Dad Is a "Reel" Catch!

Materials

6-12" (15-30 cm) stick or dowel
6-12" (15-30 cm) length of string or heavy gauge fishing line
round ring
paper clip
tagboard
fine-tipped markers or colored pencils
sandpaper
odorless varnish or shellac
paintbrush

Let's Make It

1. Have children find their own "fishing poles"—lengths of stick or dowel. Children can strip the bark from their sticks and use sandpaper to make them smooth.
2. With adult assistance, children can paint varnish on their poles in an outdoor area. Be sure to use varnish only with supervision, in an outdoor area. Children should leave the area as soon as they complete their task. Leave the poles to dry thoroughly.
3. Have each child measure and cut a length of fishing line. Tie one end of the line to the pole. A dab of glue can be used to keep the line firmly in place.
4. Attach a paper clip, ring, or similar fitting to the end of the line. This can be decorated to look like a fishing lure if desired.
5. Children can draw and cut fish from tagboard. Remember, fish come in all shapes and sizes!
6. Have children copy the following message on one side of their fish.

Happy Father's Day, Daddy
You're a reel catch!
Love, _____

7. Have each child punch a hole near the fish mouth and attach a paper clip that can be hooked to the "fishing hook."

by Robynne Eagan

117

Personalized Key Chain for Dad

Materials
- construction paper
- tagboard
- pencil
- scissors
- hole punch
- white craft glue and glue brush
- sandpaper
- sealer product (i.e. acrylic varnish or Mod Podge™)
- key chain (can be found at craft supply stores)
- photo (optional)

Let's Make It
1. Choose a small photo or draw something that means something special to your dad. Shape the photo or design into the simplest shape possible.
2. Lay the shape on tagboard. Trace it and cut out a template shape.
3. Trace the shape on construction paper many times, depending upon how thick you want the key chain decorator to be.
4. Punch a hole in the same spot on each shape.
5. Paint a thin coat of glue on the top of each paper shape and begin layering the shapes one on top of the other. You can arrange the layers by color for added effect. Place the photo or hand-drawn design on top.
6. Put something heavy on top of the stack and allow it to dry overnight.
7. Once dry, sand the edges and apply a thin coat of sealer product. Additional coats can be added if desired.
8. Add the key chain and wrap it for dad.

Father's Day Tack

A one-of-a-kind tack for coats, ties, or caps.

Materials
- Sculpey III™ clay
- tie tack back (can be found at craft or bead shops)

Let's Make It
1. Roll a popcorn-sized piece of clay into the shape of something dear to your dad: your face, a dog's face, a golf ball, a baseball, a fish, or whatever. Keep it simple, as it needs to be very small.
2. Press the shape securely onto the flat face of the tie tack. You may need to reshape it a little.
3. Press details onto the surface of your design.
4. Bake the tacks after class or have an adult volunteer to do this for you according to the directions given for the clay you use.
5. Allow it to cool before wrapping it for Dad.

by Robynne Eagan

Pop-Out Father's Day Card (Front)

fold →

1. Use reproducible sheets for the front and inside of cards.
2. Use construction paper or lightweight cardboard for the cards. Color the pictures.
3. Use construction paper or lightweight cardboard for "pop-outs."
4. Paste "pop-outs" on cards on the places marked with Xs.

by Sister M. Yvonne Moran

Pop-Out Father's Day Card (Inside)

Dear Dad,

Have fun on Father's Day.
This is my wish—
I hope you can go to your favorite spot
And catch a great big FISH.

Happy Father's Day!

For a Dear Dad

Even though the school year is nearly over, let's not forget to make a special surprise for Dad on Father's Day. Any one of the following gift projects is sure to be something your students will enjoy making— and Dad will love to receive it on his special day!

Family Photo Bookmark

Materials

construction paper
photographs
clear adhesive paper
   (2" clear packing tape can be substituted)
decorative edging shears
glue
felt tip pens
ruler

Directions

1. Have each child bring in several family photos that do not need to be returned. Instruct children to cut people and pets from these photos.

2. Cut the construction paper into 2" x 7" strips, then let the students glue their photo cut-outs to the strips. Allow to dry.

3. Cover each photo strip with clear adhesive. Smooth out any bubbles with the side of a ruler.

4. Have children trim the edges of their bookmarks with decorative edging shears. Next, have each child write a message for Dad on the back and sign his or her name.

Initial Eyeglass Case

Materials

felt
jute twine
markers
glue
scissors
decorative edging shears
ruler

Directions

1. Use the edging shears to cut a 7" felt square for each child.

2. Show children how to fold the square in half, then glue the long side and one short side together to form the glass case.

3. Have students use a marker to print their father's first initial on the front of the case.

4. Have students trace the initial with glue, then help them cut pieces of twine and set them in the glue. Allow glue to dry.

by Marie E. Cecchini

Designer Hankies

Materials

men's handkerchiefs
permanent markers
corrugated cardboard
stapler
utility knife (adult use)

Directions

1. Use the utility knife to cut several large squares of corrugated cardboard.

2. Staple a handkerchief to each of the cardboard squares. This will keep the fabric taut while students decorate the handkerchiefs.

3. Let students use permanent markers to create their own Father's Day designs on their handkerchiefs.

Pot of Gold Change Dish

Materials

baker's clay
gold acrylic paint or white tempera
  mixed with gold glitter
paint brushes

Directions

1. Prepare baker's clay by mixing 4 cups flour and 1 cup salt with $1^1/2$ cups water. Knead the mixture until smooth, adding a small amount of water if the clay is too stiff.

2. Have children mold the clay into small pinch pots. Allow pots to air dry, or bake them at 300°F for about one hour.

3. Let children paint their pots with gold acrylic paint (a little goes a long way), or use a mixture of white tempera and gold glitter.

by Marie E. Cecchini

Hats Off to Dad

Materials

plain white baseball or painter's cap
fabric paints
gift card
tissue paper

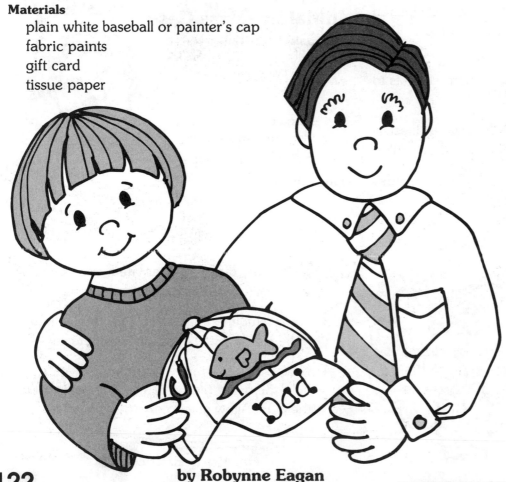

Let's Make It

1. Allow children to practice using the various fabric paints on a sample piece of canvas.

2. Have children write their name inside of the hat on a line that reads "_____'s Dad."

3. Let children decorate Dad's hat any way that they choose.

4. Allow hats to dry before moving.

5. Have children wrap the hats in tissue.

6. Have children complete a gift card below and attach it to the gift.

by Robynne Eagan

Patriotic Wind Sock

This is an easy-to-make craft that your students
will be proud to display on July 4th!

Materials

blue construction paper, 8" x 8" sheets
white construction paper for stars and 1" stripes
red construction paper for 1" stripes
star pattern on this page
crayons or markers
glue
scissors
hole punch
yarn

Directions

One sheet of blue construction paper will make the body of the wind sock. Using the star pattern, have the students trace and cut out stars from white construction paper and glue on the body of the wind sock.

Alternate red and white 1" stripes along the inside bottom edge of the wind sock, gluing or stapling them to the edge.

Roll the sock into a tube and glue or staple together. Punch a hole on each side of the wind sock and attach a length of yarn with which to hang it.

by Mary Tucker

American Flag

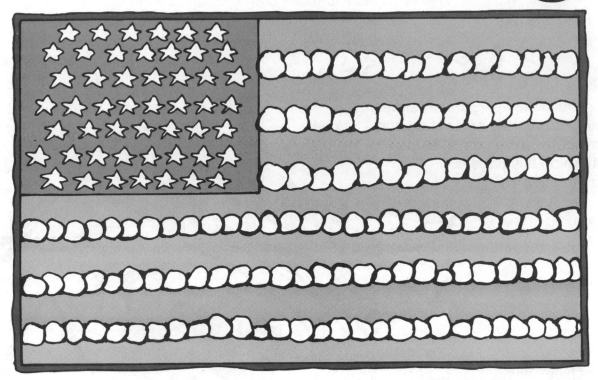

Materials

large paper grocery bag
red and blue tempera paint
white cotton balls (approximately 96)
50 silver or white star stickers
pencil, scissors, glue

Procedure

1. Cut one panel (17" x 13") from a large paper grocery bag. This will be the flag.

2. Cut a 6¹/₂" x 6" rectangle from the remaining part of the bag. Set it aside. This will be the background for the stars.

3. With the large panel in a horizontal position, outline a 6¹/₂" x 6" rectangle in the upper left corner for the stars.

4. Draw 13 horizontal 1" stripes.

5. Paint the entire large panel red. (You will still be able to see the pencil marks you made.) Paint the small rectangle blue.

6. Allow paint to dry several hours, then glue the blue rectangle in place on the flag. (If the paper curls put it under a thick book overnight to flatten it.)

7. Glue cotton balls in a row on every other stripe, beginning with the second stripe.

8. Attach 50 star stickers on the blue rectangle, arranging them so they are spaced evenly. (Preschoolers will stick stars at random unless you direct them otherwise. Older children should be able to put stars in rows.)

Variations for Older Grades

- Study the different types of flags that were used to represent the United States of America throughout history. Divide the class into groups and have each group make a different flag.

- Find pictures of the Presidents who served under various flags, and hang their pictures next to the corresponding flags.

by Maria B. Smith

Happy Birthday, USA!

Advance Preparation: Cut a 6" x 18" piece of white paper for each child. Cut nine red and blue paper candles (½" x 2") for each child. Put glitter in saltshakers to make it easier for children to use.

Get

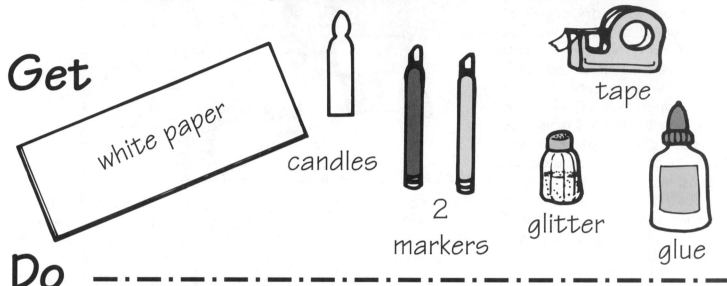

white paper

candles

2 markers

glitter

glue

tape

Do

1. Color and write.

2. Turn over and glue.

3. Glitter.

4. Tape.

Happy Birthday, USA!

by Carol Ann Bloom

"Revolutionary" Activities

Revolutionary Soldier

Take a cardboard toilet paper tube and paint the bottom half blue. When dry, crisscross two white strips of vinyl or cloth adhesive tape across the bottom half of the tube. With markers, create a face on the upper half of the tube. Cut two small strips from blue construction paper and attach one to each side for arms. Make three 2¹/₂" curved strips from blue construction paper and staple together to make the soldier's three-cornered hat.

Woven Place Mats

Have the students do a paper weaving craft to make their party place mat. This mat will be a flag replica. Fold a white sheet of construction paper (9" x 12") in half lengthwise. Teachers need to draw straight lines about 2" from the cut edges. The children will cut a series of parallel slits from the folded edge to the teacher's guide line. Open the paper flat and proceed to weave red and white strips of paper in and out of the slits. Each strip will alternately go over and under the paper. Next, cut a blue square to be glued in the upper left corner. Use adhesive stars. Tape the ends of the woven strips down to secure.

Note: Betsy Ross' flag had 13 stars representing the 13 colonies. They were placed in a field of blue.

Noisemakers

Use clean aluminum soft drink cans. Place a handful of dried beans or popcorn kernels into the can; tape the opening shut. Completely cover each can with aluminum foil. Decorate with sticker stars and shake, shake, shake!

Sparkling Fireworks

Start with a sheet of black construction paper. With a hole punch, punch circles from different colors of construction paper. Glue circles in a cluster in the center of the black paper. Then use glue to draw lines leaving the circles in a swirl design. Sprinkle glitter over the paper, shaking off the excess. Now you have a picture to celebrate patriotic fireworks bursting in the night sky.

WATERMELON Crafts

Paper Plate Watermelon

Materials
- one paper plate per child
- pink, green, and black tempera paint
- scissors

Paint the outside edge of the paper plate green for the rind. Paint the inside of the plate pink. When dry, make the seeds using black paint. For small children, you may have to make a cardboard stencil to paint on the seeds. Cut the watermelon in halves or fourths to teach simple fractions.

Watermelon Seed Art

Materials
- paper
- glue
- lots of watermelon seeds

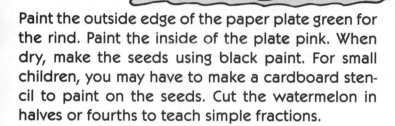

Let the students' imaginations go wild on this project. Have the children design their own seed people, animals, flowers, and strange creatures. Work in small groups to add cooperation to this lesson.

Watermelon Flags

Materials
- lots of watermelon seeds
- white paper 8$\frac{1}{2}$" x 11"
- blue tempera paint
- red tempera paint

Cut the white paper into the shape of a watermelon. Make a flag design on the paper with a pencil. Draw stars in the upper left corner and stripes going horizontally across the watermelon shape. Paint some of the seeds red and the others blue. Glue the blue seeds on the watermelon flag for stars and the red ones across the flag to make the stripes. Leave the white stripes blank. Hang these on a bulletin board display with the caption *The USA is really "ripe" for me.*

Watermelon People

Materials
- whole watermelon
- yarn, lace, old hats, shirts, and so on
- paper or paint for facial features

Dress the watermelon to look like a person. If you are fortunate enough to have more than one watermelon, turn the activity into a contest. Name each watermelon person, and write creative stories about the lives of the watermelon people. Stress the importance of who, what, where, when, and why.

by Jo Jo Cavalline and Jo Anne O'Donnell

127

Ocean in a Bottle

Materials

- clear plastic bottle (water bottles work great)
- blue food coloring
- glitter, tiny shells, tiny stones
- plastic or rubber sea creatures
- pouring instruments (cup with spout or funnel)
- eyedropper
- muffin tin
- puffy paints in glittery blue and white, and a paintbrush (optional)

Let's Make It

1. Cover a work area with vinyl or work inside an empty water table.

2. Fill muffin cups with various ocean items.

3. Have children fill the bottles about three-fourths of the way with water.

4. Let children use the eyedropper to add blue food coloring to the water until the desired shade is achieved.

5. Children can create their own "ocean" by adding glitter and other ocean items such as shells or stones to the water. When the ocean has been created, the lid of the bottle should be tightly sealed by an adult.

6. The outside of the bottle can be decorated with puffy blue and white fabric paints to look like ocean waves.

Beach in a Bag

Materials

- freezer bags
- refined sand
- seashells, starfish, worn glass, driftwood twigs, and pebbles
- spoons for scooping sand
- labels for names and decoration
- fine-tipped markers

Let's Make It

1. Have children fill their bags about halfway with sand.

2. Have children add items to the bag to create their own beach.

3. Have children decorate labels to read "_____'s Beach."

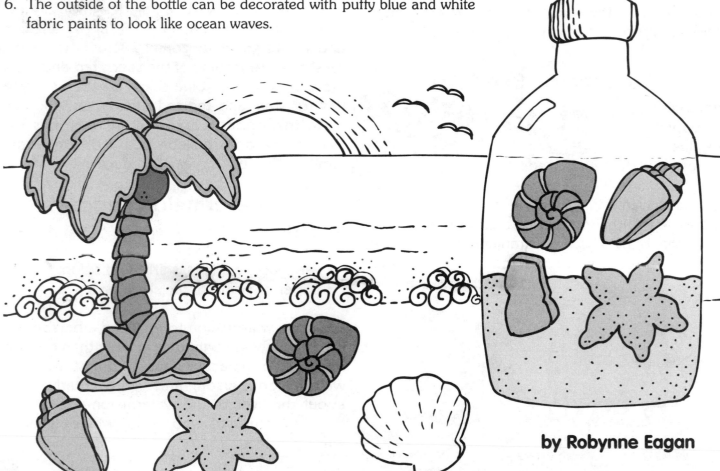

by Robynne Eagan